...ce and Inf...

D1629725

4000000130173 0

Home for Christmas

Alice Taylor

I love Christmas. It's a love affair that began in childhood and never faded. Where I grew up, on a farm in the hills of north Cork, Christmas revolved around the home. My mother created memorable Christmases. She believed in the sacredness of the season and celebrated it with respect for its origins. She prepared for it as for a royal visit. This is what I learned from her. Now I celebrate in a similar way here in my home in Innishannon. Our Christmas memories, like young trees, are planted in childhood and over the years sprout many branches. That memory tree has grown branches that for me trace the changing face of Christmas down through the decades.

RECENT BOOKS BY ALICE TAYLOR

And Time Stood Still
The Gift of a Garden
Do You Remember?
The Women
Tea and Talk

For a complete list see www.obrien.ie

Home for Christmas

Alice Taylor

Photographs by Emma Byrne

BRANDON

First published 2017 by Brandon,
an imprint of The O'Brien Press Ltd,
12 Terenure Road East, Rathgar,
Dublin 6, D06 HD27, Ireland
Tel: +353 1 4923333; Fax: +353 1 4922777
E-mail: books@obrien.ie
Website: www.obrien.ie
The O'Brien Press is a member of Publishing Ireland.

ISBN: 978-1-84717-965-4

Parts of this text were first published as *The Night before Christmas*,
but have been substantially rewritten and incorporated into this
new text.
Text © Alice Taylor 2017
Photographs © Emma Byrne
Typesetting, layout, editing, design © The O'Brien Press Ltd

10 9 8 7 6 5 4 3 2 1
21 20 19 18 17

Printed and bound in Poland by Białostockie Zakłady Graficzne S.A.
The paper in this book is produced using pulp from managed forests.

Published in
DUBLIN
UNESCO
City of Literature

Dedication

For my mother, Lena Taylor,
and all mothers who nurtured the sacred seeds of Christmas
in the hearts of their children

Contents

'Away in a Manger'

Christmas was a warm glow that shone through the cold winter of our school days. Come December, its lights began to twinkle invitingly from a far distant horizon and a sense of anticipation kept us trudging on determinedly in its direction. A bright contrast to the rest of the year, its radiance spread far wider that its allotted twelve days. Like the beacon of a lighthouse, Christmas shone across those bleak winter days drawing us invitingly towards its warm heart.

Down through the years that Christmas glow has never faded for me. It all began in an old-fashioned farmhouse from where we walked daily across the fields to a small two-roomed school looking across the river valley at the Kerry mountains. A Christmas candle was lit there that still glows warmly in my heart.

Going to school was a sentence inflicted on us in childhood during what would otherwise have been days of freedom. Adults constantly assured us that we were swimming through seas of ignorance to reach the desirable shore of being educated, and in our struggle across these seas of ignorance there were three islands of reprieve – namely, the school holidays. These kept us going, even when the waters between them were not to our liking. First came the Easter holidays, and, though darkened by the shadows of Lenten fasting, they were redeemed by Easter Sunday, with the return to eating sweets and with the arrival of baby calves and of bluebells beneath the trees in the nearby fort.

Then it was a short span to reach the summer-holiday island, with its long warm days of haymaking and swimming in the river down by the meadows. But when summer ended, there was a long, long, cold stretch to reach the Christmas island, and there were hazardous waters to cross – waters of tumbling brown torrents, muddy gaps, dripping trees and soaking wet boots, freezing mornings, frozen fingers and toes with chilblains. The Christmas island seemed almost unreachable as we journeyed across grey frosty fields or through driving rain to arrive, soaking wet with chilled bodies, to sit in an unheated classroom until evening.

In our two-roomed school there were two fires: one in the master's room, which heated the chimney, and the other in the smaller children's room, where an ancient range coughed out black smoke. On this we warmed our bottles of milk before going out into the play yard, where we ran around, having hunts and cat-and-mouse games to warm our freezing extremities. Before the range had heated itself up properly it was time to go home, and by then the air in the room, fanned by tall rattling windows and holes in the timber floor, had only just come up above zero degrees.

The thought of Christmas approaching was like a warm candle glowing in the distance. Would we survive until then? Sometimes it seemed like a mirage in the distance. Was it real? Would it ever come? The master kept us guessing as to when we would actually get our holidays, and I worried that Christmas would somehow pass us all by and never call to our school. Could we be left marooned in our frozen corner?

Then a miracle happened. A new teacher came to replace one of the regular ones. She was young, bright and beautiful, and like a brilliant butterfly she brought colour and vibrancy into the grey world of winter. We soaked it up like dry sponges. She sang and danced and introduced us to the wonders of the tuning fork, which we viewed as if it were a magic wand. She struck it smartly off the edge of the desk, and it hit a note that was supposed to somehow launch us into a musical air. There was many a false start and crash landing, but eventually we took off.

With the arrival of December, our teacher talked constantly about the approaching Christmas. Then, wonder of wonders, she decided to teach us a Christmas carol. Up to then, carols were confined to the radio or to the church choir on Christmas morning. They were not part of our normal school curriculum, and our singing repertoire was limited to 'do, re, mi'

and songs with a nationalistic flavour. This Christmas angel decided that our repertoire should be stretched to include a seasonal item. Christmas would not go unheralded, she proclaimed. We were delighted.

Her choice of carol was inspired: 'Away in a Manger' was perfect for our farming background – this carol was speaking our language. That evening I arrived home bearing a grubby copybook into which the words of 'Away in a Manger' had been laboriously copied. My brother Tim, who had a wonderful tenor voice and who was part of the local church choir, was a great help. When he launched into 'Away in a Manger', we heard the heights to which our teacher was trying to raise us. Assisted by our neighbour Bill, who came every night to help with our lessons, we diligently learnt the words, and they became imprinted into my memory.

The 'Manger' got a fair mangling in our original renditions, but our young teacher was blessed with the power of positive thinking, and slowly but surely we began to sound almost bearable. We knew by her face when we began to achieve notes that were less jarring and eventually grasped a bit of the rhythm. Well, at least most of us did. Our conductor believed in inclusiveness, and in her world there were no such people as non-singers. We were all potential nightingales, she assured us, and refinement would come with practice. And practise we did. She lifted us up into musical spheres previously undreamed of not to mention unattainable.

Every day in school I eagerly looked forward to the singing class. It was the last class of the day, and when you are just ten years old that is a long, long wait. At last singing class arrived. After striking her magic fork off the desk, our teacher stood in front of us waving a conductor's baton. As far as we were concerned she might as well have been brandishing a bread knife, but so enthusiastic and joyful was her approach that within minutes she had us all fired up and trying desperately to get the rhythm.

Then, miraculously, one day a breakthrough came. We were actually singing tunefully. The teacher might have been conducting with a baton, but to us she was waving a magic wand that was transforming the stable in our farmyard into a cave on a hillside in Bethlehem, our manger into the manger in Bethlehem.

With every wave of her baton she wove magic through the air, and my picture of the stable became clearer and clearer. The baby Jesus was lying on the hay, with Mary and Joseph kneeling beside him and the shepherds watching silently from the shadows. Angels floated through the night sky and swept in through the high windows of the stable, and sheep came up from the fields and in the stable door. Our two farm horses, Paddy and James, were transformed into a friendly grey donkey and a brown cow contentedly chewing the cud. Christmas had come into our stable. Christmas was coming home to our farm.

For me, that carol 'Away in a Manger' has never lost its magic. It is our old stable, the baby Jesus, a grey donkey, a brown cow, sheep coming in the door and angels floating through the air. It's home, it's Bethlehem, and it's Christmas.

Getting ready for Christmas on the farm began with bringing the heifers up from the fields by the river into the warmth of the stalls for the winter. Grass was no longer growing, and, as the land became softer after persistent rain, the animals could cut it up. Also, they needed sheltered housing during the cold winter months.

My father might have thought that all this was necessary, but the heifers had other ideas. They had enjoyed free-range roaming facilities all along the banks of the river since they arrived as lovable baby calves in early May. Now they were no longer lovable babies but rampaging teenagers with one common bond – and that was to do things their way. Their way was not my father's way, which, on the day of their enforced return up through the hilly fields to the farmyard, led to a bellowing confrontation between man and animal.

It would prove to be a battle of wills. The heifers were young, wild, strong-willed and determined to resist any stop put to their gallop. And gallop they did. When they succeeded in breaking free of our encircling army, they took off at full speed with tails flying high, heading back down to the river bank. My father shot after them with a tirade of colourful profanities that were enough to set fire to the sods of earth flying high behind them.

Once ensconced in their desired location under the trees along by the river, they eyed us from beneath the bare branches with frothing mouths, swishing tails, stamping hooves and wild eyes. They were formidable opponents, girding themselves for the next assault. But there was one weakness in their position. Backed by the trees and the deep river, they had no retreat so were open to frontal attack. My father, their arch-enemy, reassembled his army, and the military manoeuvre began again.

Slowly, the opposing army surrounded the encamped army, endeavouring to block off all means of escape. We were positioned at different gaps up along the fields from the river to the farmyard. No general issued orders with the same exactitude as my father, intent on hemming in the heifers from all angles. You needed to know your field history to be able to follow his instructions: 'Aliceen, will you block off Matty's

Gap?' and 'Phileen, will you cover Jack Free's Hole?'

Knowing our terrain, we understood perfectly, but trying to outrun a four-legged young heifer who had the speed of an Olympian was another matter altogether. If they outran us, our commander-in-chief spared no details as to our ineptitude, and if we outran them, we were confronted by a wild-eyed snorting heifer contemplating tossing us into the air out of her path. One outcome could leave you physically dead, and the alternative could lead to mental annihilation.

After many breaks for freedom, during which both armies advanced and retreated, the heifers were frog-marched as far as the stall doors. They peered with wild-eyed terror into the dark depths of the ancient stone stall. To them, after months enjoying fields of freedom along by the river, these were the gates of Hell. And we were the Devil incarnate. We held our ground and, by sheer physical force, edged them forward until their heads slipped between the stalls, which we quickly snapped shut. By then the heifers were exhausted – and so was Dad's Army.

It was a stormy start to our Christmas preparations, but after that things calmed down. The sheep were light-footed so did little damage to the land over winter, and their thick fleecy coats protected them from the winter cold. As on the first Christmas night, they alone were out in the fields. Around the farmyard the work had eased because much of the livestock had been sold off before Christmas. The pigs had gone to market, as had the geese and ducks, so the hens alone remained to be fed. The farmyard rested. The animal world too was preparing for Christmas.

Holly Sunday

Amajor safari was undertaken a few weeks before Christmas when the eagerly awaited Holly Sunday arrived. We set out, with balls of foxy binder twine, a saw and a hatchet, to bring home the holly – the refinement of a pruner had yet to find its way into the depths of rural Ireland. Collecting the holly was our first step in the preparations for Christmas. Our suppressed, simmering anticipation was at last free to boil over because the door into the wonder of Christmas had swung open.

We trudged through stubble-stiffened fields, through fields of saturated grass and through sprouting green rushes and waded through muddy gaps laden with puddles of winter rain. Finally we reached the river that was the boundary running along the valley between us and a neighbouring farm. We got across this river by skilfully balancing on top of the large stepping stones put in position by our neighbour Bill. Having acquired our balance on the first stone, we then jumped onto the next one, where we did the same balancing act, and mercifully reached the other side without losing our footing and toppling into the swirling water.

Then up many hilly fields and across thorny ditches

until we reached the wood. Here we did a tour of inspection along the edges of the wood, trying to locate the tree with the best red berries. Sometimes the birds had beaten us to it so we had to go deeper into the wood until we were all satisfied as to which was the best holly tree. Then we brought the saw into action and cut down a profusion of berried branches. Sometimes, if a branch proved too stubborn, the crack of the hatchet brought it into final submission. If my father, who was a protector of trees, had been with us, he would soon have put a stop to our tree-mauling. All the holly was collected into thorny heaps, then it was tied with the binder twine into firm bundles and swung over our shoulders.

The journey home was more hazardous because our river balancing act was encumbered by the bundles of holly on our backs. But years of precarious ditch-climbing and river-crossing had honed our athletic skills, so, after a few near misses, we reached the other bank safely. On arrival, we carried the bundles of holly to the old turf house at the end of the yard, which had been washed out in preparation for the geese whose plucked bodies would soon hang there.

Before the geese could be plucked, the grisly business of execution was undertaken by my mother, who did it quietly behind closed doors. Then we all sat down with a still-warm goose across our knees, and plucking commenced. Feathers and white down fluttered all over us and turned us into snow children as the tea chest in the middle of the circle between us gradually filled to overflowing. The feathers and down were later used to fill pillows and feather ticks. (Duvets had yet to float into our bedrooms.) The goose wings had their knuckles seasoned by the fire and were then used as dust collectors on the stairs or tied to a long handle to collect high-flying cobwebs.

The plucked geese were hung off the rafters in the old stone turf house. Here they swung, heads downwards, like fallen angels. Peering in at their grey, ghost-like figures in the semi-darkness, through a gap in the battered wooden door, had the same scaring effect as ghost stories told around the fire late at night. Some of these geese would go to town cousins, and three were for our own festive consumption on Christmas Day, New Year's Day and Little Christmas.

Preparation of the yard and house were next on the agenda. Work began outside. All the outhouses and walls were whitewashed or cement-washed, and the yards were given a good brushing. Then attention was given to the inside of the house. Black Ned came to clean the chimney, and we children were convinced that he was getting it ready for Santa. Today, when my chimney cleaner Tim comes, he is armed with a vacuum cleaner, and I do not see even a trace of soot in the entire process. Back then, not so. The giant operation of cleaning the chimney brought the whole house to a standstill. It was the one day of the year when the fire, our only source of heat and our only means of cooking, was out of action. Soot billowed down when Ned pushed his brushes up the wide chimney, screwing on additions as the handles disappeared from view. The billowing soot, as well as filling the fireplace, swirled out over the entire kitchen like a blanket of black snow. Job done, Ned wrapped up his sticks and, looking a little blacker than when he arrived, disappeared out the gate.

Then the big clean-up began. The hob was white-washed, and it was a matter of pride to have the line dividing the black smoke channel from the white-washed area be straight. Everything in the kitchen had to be washed and scrubbed. The kitchen table and chairs were scrubbed white from a tin bucket of hot water laced with washing soda. If the morning happened to be fine, the chairs were carried to the spout at the end of the yard where they could get a better scrubbing under the flowing water. Finally, the cement kitchen floor was scrubbed clean with a deck brush. We were ready for a health-and-safety inspection if they had been in vogue at the time.

All the bedrooms got a scrubbing and a polishing too, which was no small job as those were the days

of timber floors or linoleum. I can remember skating across the linoleum with worn knickers under my bare feet, the better to effect a good shine. This was the real beginning of getting ready for Christmas. It took days before things got back to normal.

Cleaning the windows was my regular household job. Every Saturday throughout the year I was supplied with newspaper dipped in paraffin oil to do the kitchen windows, but come Christmas my responsibilities extended to all the windows of the house. I enjoyed the undertaking, feeling that Santa would appreciate my clean windows. I must have thought he was a hygiene inspector.

Traces of that belief must still remain with me because to get ready for Christmas now I give the house an overhaul. And, as on the farm, I begin outside. The first step in my preparations for Christmas is putting the garden to bed. Maybe, for me, the garden is my farm. I cut back all the perennials no longer looking good and push those who do not like Jack Frost into shady corners. One year I left this job until after Christmas, believing that there would be no hard frost until January. Boy, was that a mistake. I lost all my beautiful Cannas, which turned into brown mush overnight. A lesson never to be forgotten.

There is no teacher like experience, as I learnt from my father when I questioned the need for the spare block of unused hay that stood in our barn every year when the feeding season ended and the cows were let out again after winter. In his first year running the farm, at the age of sixteen, after his father had died, he ran out of hay, and he had never forgotten the sound of hungry animals. Like my father, I learnt from experience. I will never forget the minus-ten-degree winter of 2009. So, around the yard and garden, everything that needs frost protection is covered. The garden paths and the yard are swept clean, and, when all the pots are bedded down for the winter, I bring out the hose and wash down the backyard. All is now well on my little farm.

Green Gifts

As a young lad, Uncle Jacky planted a holly tree in his garden. In fact, the very first tree he planted was a holly tree. Then he planted an apple tree. Uncle Jacky's knowledge of gardening was acquired from a very austere Protestant lady who lived outside Innishannon village in a large rambling old house surrounded by an extensive garden. She needed an energetic young lad to help her to maintain this amazing garden. Uncle Jacky was willing and able, so he was the ideal man for the job. At home money was scarce, and his mother had opened a little village shop to help pay the bills. He was glad to help out with the little extra money that he got from this thrifty old lady.

Years later, he would smile when he recalled that no expense was too much for the garden but that the woman did not apply the same philosophy in other directions. But what she passed on in gardening expertise was priceless. She was an expert in grafting, slipping and making a little go a long way. A mistress of 'waste not want not', her garden also supplied her kitchen. The Chelsea Flower Show was her annual outing.

Uncle Jacky was not the only man at work in her garden. She also had an old gardener who had been with her for years, and who, as a result of decades of practical experience, was as knowledgeable as the Royal Horticultural Society encyclopedia. Uncle Jacky was an enthusiastic and energetic absorber of their gardening knowledge. From the woman and old Tom he mastered the art of cultivating food for the kitchen table while still having a garden that was a visual delight.

Now, over one hundred years later, his apple tree and his holly tree are still standing, now part of my garden. While the apple tree holds central position and is the queen of the garden, the staunch holly stands beside her and sometimes shoulders her out of its way. Every year in April and May the apple tree bursts into gorgeous blossoms that float to the ground in a pink swirl. When autumn comes, overripe apples thud to the ground, bursting into sloppy mush and making a feast for birds, bees and anything that can fly or crawl. Then the queen, having changed her clothing for every season, sheds her coat and goes to sleep for the winter.

The sensible holly, on the other hand, does not waste her energy changing her clothes for any season but keeps standing firm in the same sturdy outfit in all weathers. She is a slow grower, but, come high winds or hard frost, she holds her ground. She is of the 'I shall not be moved' brigade.

Every Christmas, I go into the garden and say, 'Thank you, Uncle Jacky.' He taught me the comfort of having your own holly tree, and for years his Golden King was the only holly tree in the garden. Now there are about five holly trees of different textures and sizes. When the deciduous trees retire for the winter, the hollies come into their own. They stand with military erectness, giving structure to the winter garden.

When planting a holly tree, it is best to make up your mind at the very beginning as to location – no messing about in indecision. Decide on location and then leave her in peace. I never ever considered shifting Uncle Jacky's Golden King holly tree. The name carries imperious royal overtones, but the curious thing is that even though she is called Golden King, she is actually a female – one of the many confusing contradictions of gardening. She remains where Uncle Jacky planted her, cheek by jowl beside the apple tree, where sometimes they get tangled together due to proximity. When this happens, I get someone who knows more than I do to engage in a bit of skilful pruning. I would not dream of trying to curb Her Royal Highness.

I learnt my lesson the hard way. Having planted a harmless little holly in what I thought was the right place – which proved, as so often happens in gardening, to be the wrong place when my little holly was no longer so little – I had the temerity to dig her up and move her. She did not like it one little bit. She threw off all her clothes in protest and turned black with temper and bad feeling. I humoured her, coaxed her, watered her, fed her and loved her back to life. Now she is a powerful, glossy lady who occasionally flashes red berries across her dark leaves like a dusky model wearing bright red lipstick.

She would put manners on you were you to think that you could take a red berry twig from her without first togging out in military garb. The Golden King is a far more benign lady, but my cranky dame is a wonderful Christmas decorator. She might be sharp and edgy, with spikes that could mortally wound you, but once in position her leaves glisten along the top edges of the dresser and around the kitchen, holding their red berry glow when the poor old King has long given up her bounce.

The late Brian Cross, that connoisseur of gardening who inspired so many ignoramuses like me, advised pruning your holly at Christmas as you decorated your home. What a sound piece of advice, and every Christmas, I say, 'Thank you, Brian,' for his wise direction. His was the first open garden I ever visited, and to say that I was taken aback at its wonder and profusion is to put it mildly. Uncle Jacky was long gone, and I was struggling with my ignorance and inability to cope in his garden. When I returned home, I apologised to Uncle Jacky at his garden gate for my lack of gardening expertise and application, and promised to try harder. And I did. I was beginning to learn that a garden is a thing of beauty and a job forever.

With the approach of Christmas, I meander around the garden and cast an appraising eye over my holly trees. They return my gaze with glossy green stares of defiance, brazenly telling me to make up my mind as to shape and quantity of requirements before I dare point a pruner in their direction. Back in a time of deep gardening ignorance, when I fancied myself as a tree surgeon, I pruned the leg of the Golden King too bare and too high. I was trying to turn her from a flouncy lady into a long-legged ballerina. Not one of my brightest ideas. She looked like a long-legged, tormented teenager in a scandalously short miniskirt.

She escapes any serious thinning of her tresses now because they are far above reach. In order to get at her berried branches, a tall stepladder would be required, and a wise friend of mine has advised that any person over sixty should not mount a wobbly stepladder. Or any stepladder. So the Golden King smirks down at me, mouthing 'Good enough for you', and peers around at the other holly trees from her lofty location, grinning with derision at their plight. From her high perch she is out of reach of my wandering pruner.

I wait for a dry day to do my holly gathering. If the cutting of each holly branch drenches you in a cold shower, then pruning and gathering holly is not a pleasant exercise. But on a dry, sunny or even frosty morning it can be very therapeutic. So, come a dry morning, I seize the day. As I do the rounds, armed with a large laundry basket and pruner, I recall the occasion on which each tree was planted. I acknowledge the pleasure that each tree has given me over the years. Each tree in your garden is part of your life.

Many trips are made back and forth between the garden and the back porch where each holly cargo is tumbled out. One Christmas, as we gathered holly, my sister Ellen, home from Canada, declared, 'Al, if you were in Toronto, all this would cost you a fortune.' From experience, I err on the side of abundance because invariably once decorating begins you could run short of supply and have to dash into the garden for more. The decorating day could well be deluging rain or freezing cold and then I would regret my earlier Scrooge miserliness.

Holly gathered, I walk the garden and survey the after-effects on the holly trees. They looked slimmer and trimmer, like ladies who have been to Weight Watchers. Then it is time to come inside where the kitchen is first on the hit list. I cast a beady eye over my two dressers that flank the Aga and decide that they

both need a serious overhaul. It is no small job. Then I say, 'God bless the man or woman who invented the dishwasher.' What a blessing to the kitchen fraternity. Off comes everything displayed on the dresser shelves, straight into the dishwasher.

The large jugs and dishes along the top are immersed in the long Belfast sink which I had the foresight to install years previously in a kitchen overhaul. When all the empty shelves have had their faces washed, then the big return begins. The dressers are a full day's job, but once done that is the back broken in the kitchen overhaul. The rest of the kitchen work is tidying away the clutter that accompanies everyday living.

When the kitchen is looking good, I feel that I have a clean base from which to operate. Feng Shui experts tell us that if you tidy your house you tidy your mind. Once the kitchen is tidy it inspires me to keep going. Inside me, I feel sure, is a tidy woman who has been fighting all her life to break out, but life has worked against her. Being a hoarder and a collector does not lead to minimalist living, so in the days of getting ready for Christmas my dishwasher and washing machine both have a busy time. But eventually all is to my satisfaction, and I feel that garden, yard and house are ready for Christmas.

With Christmas on its way, the furniture in the *seomra ciúin* (the quiet room) is arranged to face the fire. This is an old-fashioned fire, not electric, not gas, nor is the fire hidden behind a glass door. The large log and turf baskets are retrieved from the garden shed and filled. A fire, I have discovered, has magnetic qualities that draw people to it from all corners of the house. When this room was first envisaged many years ago, and television was barred, there was a wail of dissent and a proclamation that nobody would go in there. Time, however, proved different. The fire draws people to it like bees to a honey jar.

With fires come dust, ashes and smoke, which do not lend themselves to immaculate conditions, and this means that this room is now the high-maintenance corner of the house. But it's all worth it. Fire is the comforter when it is cold outside. If you are having a bad day or have fallen out with yourself, the warmth of the fire will heal your soul.

Cakes, Puddings
and Pies

During the weeks leading up to Christmas my mother waited patiently for the Muscatel raisins to come into our local shop. Their arrival would herald that Christmas was on the horizon. But foreign climates, about which we were totally ignorant, influenced their cropping, and world events, about which we were equally in the dark, affected their shipping. So, some years, due to all these varying influences working against them, they never made it to our little corner of the world, which was a huge disappointment to my mother. On the years they did arrive, they came in deep wooden boxes, like the gifts of the Wise Men. They were big, soft and juicy, carrying within them stones that had to be extracted before use. They were the joy of my mother's Christmas baking, used for what we called 'the sweet cake'.

Into her bread pan went three or four saucers of flour, scooped out of the bag of white flour, and a teaspoon of bread soda, which she rubbed between her palms to dissolve lumps. Then a generous dollop of butter was rubbed in, and then her special Christmas fruit was added, including her prized fat juicy raisins and sultanas. My mother was not partial to currants, so they received a lesser showing. Then in went cherries, ginger and crystallised orange peel that she had chopped into little bits. We had no weighing scales so she judged by saucer, hand, eye and taste. Five or six eggs, depending on the egg production of the day, were already beaten in a bowl and a few pinches of salt had been added.

Then came the thick sour cream she had put on standby especially for this cake. She credited the success of her cake to the quality of the cream. Top-class cream resulted in a top-class cake. All was lovingly mixed together to form a firm dough and kneaded gently around the pan. To my mother, this was a coming together of the best of ingredients, and she treated it with great respect. Supplies were expensive and scarce. Then, with the palm of her hand, she flattened out her cake into the size of her bastible, the base of which she had dusted with flour. Into this she eased her creation, making sure that the fire was hot and glowing to guarantee a satisfactory result. This cake contained many of the same ingredients as a rich fruit cake, but, because it was baked in such a large bastible, it spread out and ended up as large as her usual brown and white cakes. But it was much richer, hence the name 'Mom's Sweet Cake'.

It was our Christmas cake for many years until my sister attended a cookery class in town and came home the week before Christmas bearing a fully iced heavy fruit cake. On top of it a red Santa sleighed across the whiteness. We were mesmerised – this was like something that had come from America. Up to then, Tim Barry, the baker who did all the baking in our town, had been the only one to come up with anything remotely like this. But Tim was much more into large soft seed loaves, butter loaves and big round barmbracks with soft glossy icing streaming down their sides. There was nothing soft about my sister's iced cake. It strongly resisted the first touch of our well-worn bread knife, and we soon discovered that this new arrival had to be firmly attacked to gain entry. Once broken open it held riches hitherto unsavoured in such density, and it took us a little while to realise that these riches were best taken in small portions.

A few years later, when my mother felt that I required a year in Drishane Convent, Millstreet, Co. Cork, to hone my culinary skills, I was introduced by Madame St Benignus to the challenging elements of correct Christmas cake creation. Hers was a French order of nuns, who brought with them rather compli-cated saintly names. We called her Benny.

Benny proclaimed that the first step in Christmas cake making was the lining of the cake tin. Not com-plicated, one might think. Well, think again. Benny turned it into an exercise of military precision during which she constantly told us that perfection was in the detail but that perfection was no detail. Her master plan on tin-lining was an introduction to her concept of perfection I never forgot.

The first requirement was a large sheet of brown paper and also a spread of butter or greaseproof paper, which came to the convent in huge, heavy rolls. You laid the brown paper on the table, rested your baking tin on it and then circled around the tin with a sharply pointed pencil. Next, you cut out the circle, which, if you had done the job properly, fitted snugly into the bottom of the tin. If you cut it too small, bits of your exposed cake bottom could burn, but if it was too big, your baked cake could have strips of greasy brown paper embedded in its outer layer.

Once this base was cut and fitted, it was temporarily set aside because another step had to be taken before the base was allowed to stay put. This next step, which was far more complicated than the first, was to layer the sides of the tin. You laid the side of your tin on the paper to better gauge the height and length of your wrap-around. The height of your encircling border was the height of the tin plus a bit extra, and this bit extra was then pleated back against the main paper and snipped along with a scissors, or fluted as Benny called it, so that when it went into the tin it fanned out on the bottom. Then the base lining went in on top of it and held it in place. The height of the

side lining could vary, but if, like me, you were one of the 'to be sure to be sure' brigade and you made it too deep, your tin could finish up with an all-round stand-up collar, giving it the look of an enclosed moat. Benny soon demolished my moat.

If your paper had sufficient length to go the full way around the tin, it simplified matters, but if not you had to convince two or even three pieces of strong-minded brown paper to link up. You then had a paper-sliding problem. The whole exercise necessitated great patience on our part and brought forth exasperated sighs from Benny.

Next step was the butter paper, which was the inside jacket of the tin and would be against the sides of the cake yet to be made. The same process was followed, but butter paper is much more difficult to handle than ordinary brown paper, and trying to make it do as it's told is akin to trying to keep a two-year-old sitting still for a haircut. It shifts, slips and slides, and, unless you keep a cool head, the result could be a tangle of confusion.

Benny, a woman with whom one did not trifle, insisted that the lining of the tin had to be complete before cake-making commenced. As we embarked on the marathon undertaking of making our first Christmas cake, the lined tins stood in waiting like empty coffins until the prepared body was ready to move in.

Sometimes during the undertaking I anticipated that there could be two dead bodies by the time my job was complete.

Benny ran her enormous kitchen with the skilful expertise of an army sergeant, taking no prisoners and operating a shoot-to-kill policy. Tall, well-built and athletic, she swept around her domain in a full-length, starch-crackling white apron, keeping a sharp eye on all operations. *All in the Cooking* was her kitchen bible. In retrospect, trying to teach thirty teenagers the skill of Christmas cake making must have been quite a challenge. But it did not daunt Benny.

Her Christmas cake recipe was set in stone and adhered to with no diversification. Into our bowls went half a pound of butter and half a pound of caster sugar, which we battered with a wooden spoon into a creamy consistency. To this we added six already beaten eggs and then folded in twelve ounces of sieved flour and a quarter teaspoon of baking powder. In another bowl we mixed half a pound each of raisins, currants and sultanas, two ounces of almonds and cherries, a quarter pound of peel, half a teaspoon of spice and the grated rind of one lemon. We had already cleaned the dried fruit with dry flour as Benny had question marks over the standard of hygiene in the country of origin. The mixed peel came in small, solid, wooden boxes lined with wax paper, and we sliced it into the desired size. Benny tolerated no guesswork. Precision was the name of her game. The fruit was then added to the first bowl with a quarter glass of whiskey.

Then it was time for the transfer. The tin into which such minute preparation had gone waited on the enamel-topped table beside the mixing bowl. With bowl and wooden spoon held in waterfall position, we began the big slide. If the mixture was too dry, it fell in lifeless dollops; if too thin it ran like a bad case of diarrhoea; but with the right consistency it slid like a dream during which you had to be mindful that the greaseproof-paper base did not shift or the surrounding paper walls collapse and fold under the mixture. If this calamity happened, we had to retrieve the fallen paper, which, by then, was layered with cake mixture that would burn black as soon as it hit the heat of the oven. This would take from a perfect result. And a perfect result was the aim of Benny's game. Then the cake was baked in a moderate oven for about three and a half hours. On emerging, it was blessed with another quarter glass of whiskey or a beverage of similar potency.

Benny professed that the essence of good kitchen management was the presentation of a kitchen disaster as a dining-room triumph. In fairness, she practised what she preached, and throughout the year she rescued burnt offerings and showed us how to redeem them so that they did arrive in the dining room maybe not as a triumph but at least edible. But when it came to her Christmas cakes, Benny eliminated any possibility of a kitchen disaster by rigid quality control and strict supervision. Every batch of cakes out of the ovens was faultless, not a sunken top or fallen fruit in sight. When cooled, the cakes were firmly wrapped up in butter paper and then a layer of brown paper, and tied securely with white cord.

The first batch we made was consigned to a large press in the dining room from which they were occasionally taken out to be fed from a bottle of potent-smelling liquid that had found its way through the back door of the convent, via the yard man Tim. We never queried the source of these gurgling bottles that quietly made their way down from nearby Mushera mountain, where a home brewer catered for Benny's baking requirements.

These cakes were for the house, or for the 'friends of the house'. 'Friends of the house' was an expression that the nuns used for the good neighbours who lived around the convent farm or anyone to whom they had reason to be grateful. Christmas was the time to show appreciation for round-the-year goodness. Undoubtedly the home brewer up the mountain was counted amongst the friends of the house.

We also made cakes to take home, which we iced.

Before we embarked on this Benny instilled in us the high cost of ground almonds so the making of that icing was treated as an exercise in tight-fisted economy. It began with the separation of the whites from the yolks of the eggs. This is an exercise in balancing, to contain the yolk within the shell while the white slides effortlessly down into a waiting bowl. The end result should be a perfect, unbroken yolk and a clear, untainted white.

Not a result easily achieved by the uninitiated, and Benny wailed in protest when egg whites were infiltrated with golden yellow. The yolk was used to make the almond icing and the whites for the white icing. Some of the white was brushed onto the bald head of the cake to act as an adhesive for the layer of almond icing. With the almond layer in place, the cake was left to rest for a few days, and then came the challenging undertaking of white icing. When this had set firmly, it was time to decorate. This was a hit-and-miss affair, depending on the artistic skill of the decorator. When all our cakes were complete, they were displayed around the dining room for inspection by Reverend Mother. But no matter what she thought of our efforts, we felt that we had created masterpieces.

We also made mincemeat and plum puddings. A plum pudding is far less challenging than a cake because once the ingredients are good success is assured. There is no question of a sunken top or fruit not quite making it to the surface. While all the recipes were plentiful in butter, for the mincemeat and puddings we also used suet, which came from the local butcher and had to be teased out and cut into tiny fragments. I shudder now to think what that did to our cholesterol levels.

Once I began cooking in my own home I often silently thanked Benny for the practical rudiments of cooking which she had succeeded in instilling into my uninterested teenage head. Now, like my mother, once November comes, I visit my special shop to check if their fruit has arrived. They have large juicy fruit in old-fashioned timber boxes and mixed peel floating around in a sea of gooey juice. The smell of this shop brings back memories, and there is a feeling of sheer delight in helping oneself, ladling the succulent fruit into different containers.

My first step into Christmas baking now is the making of the mincemeat because the longer it has to mature the better it gets. As soon as I arrive home with the special fruit, my large stainless-steel marmalade saucepan is landed onto the kitchen table. Into it go three-quarters of a pound of butter and a pound and a half of brown sugar, a pound of sultanas and currants, two ounces of mixed peel, six chopped apples, the juice and rind of two oranges and two

lemons, four ounces of ground almonds and a tea-spoon of mixed spice.

There is immense satisfaction mixing all these wonderful, rich, flavoursome ingredients together, and, once mixed, they are generously blessed from a bottle that has come in via my own back door, plus a good dash of rum. There is great body in rum, and it makes its presence felt in the mixture. My marma-lade saucepan is the ideal container because when the ingredients are fully mixed the heavy cover goes on and then it can be left to its own devices in the back porch for weeks, during which time the flavours of the different fruits blend and absorb into each other. To encourage togetherness it gets an occasional stir of a wooden spoon, and an added slosh of rum stimulates the Christmas spirit.

Next, the cake and the plum pudding. I roughly follow Benny's recipes, increasing the mixtures if required. For the pudding, into a large bowl go four ounces each of breadcrumbs, currants, sultanas, rai-sins, butter and brown sugar, two ounces of flour, two ounces of peel, one ounce of ground almonds, the rind and juice of an orange or lemon, one grated sour apple, a half teaspoon each of mixed spice and salt. I mix all the dry ingredients then stir in three well-beaten eggs, two tablespoons of whiskey and half a small bottle of stout. Then I divide the mixture into

greased bowls and cover them with greaseproof paper. I stand them in saucepans of boiling water and put them into the bottom oven of the Aga to steam at their leisure.

The blessing of the Aga is that it is totally sealed so not a whisper of steam escapes during the entire cooking period. When the puddings emerge they are baptised from the special bottle that looks as innocent as holy water, and, together with the cake, they await Christmas at the bottom of Aunty Peg's press.

Keeping in Touch

When I was on a visit to America recently a New Yorker heard my accent and declared with delight, 'I am Irish.' In my naivety I inquired which part of Ireland did she come from, only to be enlightened that her great-great-great (not sure how many greats) had come from Sligo. Our roots, like those of old trees, may take many twists and turns but deep down within us all is the desire to link back to our original germination. Through the year these roots may lie dormant, but Christmas awakens many memories and we feel the need for contact.

Eight generations had lived in our old farmhouse, and, like all over Ireland, many had emigrated to different parts of the world. Come Christmas, their thoughts turned homewards, and the only way to link back to their own place was with Christmas cards. There were no phones, no emails, no Skype. The American Christmas cards brought a flavour of the New World back to the old Ireland that had formed these people and that had now, for some of them, transformed itself into an enchanted land. Some cards came early, probably because many of the emigrants had reason to remember that their homeland marched to the pace of a different drum. Johnny the Post, who was our deliverer of missives, swept them out of his bag with a flourish, declaring, 'The Yanks are on the move.'

They arrived in big envelopes, some even bright red, with strips of multicoloured stamps and stickers across the top like rows of medals decorating the chests of military veterans. To us children they were manna in the desert. Bright, brash and beautiful, they shot colour into a black and white Ireland. My mother opened the envelopes slowly, with decorum and respect, as if she were unveiling a work of art. We circled her like a ring of demanding calves waiting to be fed. Our thirst to see what was inside was held in bounds only by the knowledge that beneath our mother's kind and gentle demeanour was an impregnable wall of defence, un-breachable by any tide of attack.

The top of the envelope was not torn open but was prised slowly back from the gummed edge. If the edge was not for lifting, a kitchen knife was brought to bear, eased in and slid slowly along the top. During this undertaking the contents of the envelope often shifted and rustled, further whetting our curios-ity. Finally the exit was clear, and, very slowly, out emerged the object of all our curiosity. It was greeted with open-mouthed wonder. The big, crimson, pot-bellied Santa, bristling with snow dust, had yet to penetrate rural Ireland, but here he was with a big bag of toys tumbling off his back. We were speechless with awe. My mother's face took on a peculiar look, and I was never sure if she was impressed or dismayed. Did she see this Santa as introducing into her simple world yearnings for more than it could ever give us? But the look was quickly replaced by one of curiosity as to the name of the sender and the verse.

The verse in a Christmas card was of huge significance to my mother, so much so that it became a bit of a family joke. It also turned Christmas card shopping with her into a challenge of patience.

The overseas cards had to be sent off early because if money was not free-flowing, which it was not, you had to go on a slow boat to faraway places. If you wanted your cards to wing across the skies via airmail you had to pay accordingly. The problem with this was that my mother was never on time for anything. One of her few failings was that she was no respecter of deadlines – they were totally alien to her world. She took her time, and, as a result, always arrived late.

As the last date for overseas posting appeared on the horizon, she had a clash of priorities that brought her onto the outer fringes of the stress zone – a foreign land to my mother. Even my father, who normally forged ahead, leaving her on her slow boat to China, became aware of her predicament. He decided that something had to be done, but he was certainly not

going to do it. Christmas card writing was not within his sphere of activities. He deemed it to be a daft exercise for children or people who had nothing better to be doing.

His solution was to turn to his five daughters, who were normally the source of all his problems. (His refrain, whenever he concluded that he was buried in petticoat government, was, 'God pity the man who has five daughters.') My father was not a man of pious persuasion, but that did not prevent him, in moments of desperation, invoking heavenly bodies and even the Man Himself to intervene. After a litany of saints being called on for aid, he concluded, 'Holy divine Jesus, will one of ye useless bloody women help yer mother with those cursed cards before she drives this whole bloody madhouse madder'.

Then, because he realised that what is everyone's job is nobody's job, he decided on delegation. 'Aliceen, you are always bloody wasting time reading and scribbling, will you do something useful for a change and do those goddamn cards with your mother.' So 'doing my mother's cards', as I called it, became my job. At an early age it gave me a wonderful insight into the art of card selection and allocation.

In her head, my mother had a list of the people to whom she was going to send cards, and each card was bought with that person in mind. The illustration had to be based in the reality of her own Christmas, and the verse had in some way to be relevant to the needs of the receiver. A tall order? That is exactly why the undertaking took so long. We had only two shops selling a very limited selection of Christmas cards in our small town, and she inspected and read every card in both of those shops until she came as near as possible to meeting her requirements. If she had ever made it into a modern card shop, with their mind-boggling selections, she would have had to stay overnight in order to get it all worked out to her satisfaction.

In our local town, Hallmark was not yet packing the shelves with dancing reindeers and glistening sleighs. Our palette was limited to Brian O'Higgins and other traditional scenes. But that posed no problem to my mother because, as far as she was concerned, it was all about the crib. Her Christmas was rooted in Bethlehem. If somebody were to wish my mother 'Happy Holiday', she would probably have thought that she should be packing her case to go to Ballybunion. Neither was she going to send Christmas cards of long-coated, high-hatted gentlemen accompanied by hoop-skirted and bonneted ladies singing carols, which were just as alien to her world as Santa Claus. Not one of those cards would be dispatched to her family, be they at home or across the seas — especially if they were across the seas.

Cards bought, her job was still only half done. Next came what she termed 'doing the Christmas cards'. This entailed Sunday afternoons and many nights after supper sitting under the oil lamp at the kitchen table, writing letters to all the overseas relatives. Years later, many of them talked of their delight on receiving her Christmas card as it always contained a letter full of interesting home news and little details which she knew would be of interest to them. To her, Christmas was all about connecting with extended family and friends, and this included my father's family as well as her own because she knew that there was no way he was going to put pen to paper.

Years later, when we had all left home, I usually tried to make it back to 'do her Christmas cards' with her. Her Christmas card list was long, but in doing them with her I learnt bits of family history that I might never have heard about otherwise.

The fallout from those early days is that I still frequent card shops picking out suitable cards for special people. If at all possible, I try to put in a note for those with whom this is our only yearly link. It is so lovely to receive a card with a letter enclosed, and it enriches the sending and receiving of cards. I am not talking about typed-out sheets of a family's yearly achievements plonked like business circulars into every envelope, but a short personal note, which, in this era

Seasons
Greetings

of mass production is a little bit of gold dust.

Like my mother, I now take time when opening my cards to savour them properly. I put them aside until there is sufficient time to sit down and do so with an appreciation of the effort made by the sender. A beautiful card coming out of an envelope accompanied by a meaningful message is one of the joys of Christmas. One of my friends has two of the most handsome big dogs that you ever laid eyes on and every year they bounce into my house on her large Christmas card caught in the most ha ha poses. Sometimes smothered in snow, other times peering out the door of their colourful doggy boxes. She is a superb photographer, with the eye of the professional, and her two dogs are gorgeous. Many times over the twelve days of Christmas my eye falls on her card and it brings a smile to my face. When their cards decorate your house, your friends are all around you, gathered in spirit to celebrate Christmas with you.

Christmas Reading

Santa would make his first appearance of the season in the local paper. Then known as the *Cork Examiner*, that title was perceived as too provincial and was changed to the *Irish Examiner*. At first, a little Santa peeped in at the top of the paper, and as Christmas drew nearer he grew bigger and bigger. Then the special Christmas paper, the *Holly Bough*, appeared and it was time to send Santa a letter. Writing to Santa was a serious undertaking that occupied the hours between supper and bedtime for one night. There was much arguing and mind-changing, until, assisted by Bill, the well-thumbed and grubby pages, covered in writing and crossing-out that only Santa could interpret, were stuffed into envelopes. It was my father's responsibility to post them the following day on his way to the creamery. After that it was up to Santa.

Published by the *Cork Examiner*, the *Holly Bough* found its way into every Cork home at Christmastime. My father bought the *Examiner* on his daily trips to the creamery but for some reason did not think that the *Holly Bough* should be on our list of Christmas requirements. It was my brother Tim who brought it and any additional Christmas reading matter into our house. It contained weeks of nightly reading. Though not really geared for children, we were still delighted to see it as it was a signal that Christmas was on the way.

Another welcome arrival was the Christmas edition of *Ireland's Own*. Two pages were given over to songs, and from this we learnt the words to songs for which we only had snatches up to then. When Bill came on his nightly call, we coaxed him into reading the stories in *Ireland's Own* to us. We loved to hear of the exploits of Kitty the Hare, a nosy gossipy woman who travelled from house to house around the county, distributing local news as she went. My mother did not really approve of Kitty the Hare, but we and Bill loved her.

A magazine called the *Far East* came to us via our school, where one teacher distributed it. The only bit that was of interest to us was Pudsy Ryan, who got up to all kinds of tricks in the Children's Corner. We sat on a little stone bridge on the way home from school, and one of the eldest, who had the best reading skills, kept us up to date with 'Pudsy's Diary'. The remainder of the *Far East*, however, paid very little attention to Christmas, which was very annoying.

The *Messenger*, which my mother got from a woman who ran a pub in town, was a bit more Christmassy, with its red cover, but the *Irish Catholic*, sold from a little timber hut on the way into mass, was not colourful enough for our liking. It did sometimes have a beautiful picture of the Holy Family on the front page, and that appealed to us. Our mother constantly kept us aware that that was the reason for the season.

As far as we were concerned, of all these publications, the *Holly Bough* was the best. My mother became an avid reader of it, and sometimes, late at night, when peace reigned in her kitchen, she sat by the light of the oil lamp methodically working her way through its pages. She was not a reader who dipped in and out. My father was not a fan, but Bill was, so he and my mother had long discussions about different articles when he called to see us every night. Because it had so many articles, the reading of the *Holly Bough* was often spread out over their entire Christmas. When I came to live in Innishannon, the *Holly Bough* became part of my Christmas, and Uncle Jacky and Aunty Peg also read it in great detail.

One wet Sunday between the Christmases in 1983, I had my feet up and was reading the *Holly Bough*. As I read, the thought came into my mind that it was very Cork City orientated. What about us culchies? Surely we deserved more space and more of a voice. Then I came across an article written by a Revd Mr Doherty whom I knew had been a clergyman in Innishannon before my time. I had never met him but had heard of him. Then the thought in my mind germinated. Maybe we could have a parish Christmas publication to give our parish a voice of its own? Maybe Revd Doherty would write an article for us? There were a lot of maybes. Before I had time to suppress the impulse, I wrote Revd Doherty a letter.

One of the best pieces of advice I ever received in life was to never suppress a good impulse. Do not overanalyse it because then the rational side of your brain will convince the creative side not to go with it and the dream will die. Just go with it. Within days, back came a reply from Revd Doherty to say that he would be delighted to contribute an article to our magazine. The dream was growing wings. Now for the hard graft. No dream takes off without the hard graft. I went around to a few helpful neighbours to ask if they would write articles.

There is a reluctance in us ordinary Irish people to commit ourselves to paper. Maybe the source of this is the fear that once we put something in writing there is no going back. Another problem is that most of us are afraid of upsetting the neighbours. Worrying about what people will think can often be a huge barrier against putting pen to paper or doing something that we believe is worthwhile.

Some brave souls did come on board. When the first copies of *Candlelight* were inspected, those who

Innishann...

an
33rd

Fóill
2016

Candlelight

had not come on board said, 'Is that all you wanted?'

'That is all,' we told them. 'We are not attempting to write *Ulysses*.'

Everyone assumed that *Candlelight* would appear the following year. But, as most of us know, things do not happen simply on assumption. A friend of mine has a very shrewd observation about people. He says, 'There are those who make things happen, those who watch things happen, and those who ask, "What happened?"' In our village we are blessed with quite a few people who belong in the first category. We put in more hard graft and a second edition was indeed published the following year. Our Christmas magazine has been going for many years. We have the old reliables who can be depended on to come good most years. We also have those who need to be nurtured, and we begin doing so in late summer.

Then there are those who, despite annual coaxing, never come good. They are too busy. Some of us perceive ourselves to be far busier than we really are. When confronted with the inquiry 'How long have I got to do that article?' the honest answer is, 'If you want to do it you have plenty of time, and if you do not want to do it you will never have enough time.'

Despite all kinds of ups and downs, one *Candlelight* followed another, and, over the years, it has recorded much about the parish that would have otherwise been lost. We have no big committee, just three determined women: Mary, Maureen and myself, good friends who believe in the project. Every year, the first page of *Candlelight* opens with a picture of a child holding a lighted candle – a symbol of Christmas and the beginning of a New Year. The first candle was lit in 1984.

When the idea of a parish Christmas magazine first sprouted, there was no big plan that it would go on for decades. It just did, mainly because, once launched, people loved it and wanted it to make an annual appearance. And Mary, Maureen and I believed in it.

Candlelight is posted all over the world. Last year I met a woman who had left our village many years ago, and I was amazed how familiar she was with parish happenings. When I asked how she was so well informed about village events, she told me, '*Candlelight*. It arrives every Christmas, and I look forward to it every year. It is the highlight of my Christmas.' So *Candlelight*, a bit like Kitty the Hare, goes around with the parish news and is part of our Innishannon Christmas.

Bringing the
Christmas

Growing up on a farm many years ago, the buying of Christmas presents for each other and for friends was never a problem, simply because there was no such thing as buying Christmas presents, at least not as we know them today. Santa brought presents, and that was it. No money floating around meant no presents. We never missed them, simply because we knew nothing about them.

An early sign of Christmas was the arrival of the Traveller women. Ordinarily they carried baskets full of clothes pegs, holy pictures and camphor balls. Now the baskets under their shawls took a seasonal turn, brimming over with Christmas paper chains for running across the kitchen, pleated paper skirts for the candle and big brightly coloured paper flowers. We danced around them in delight and with our enthusiasm diluted any chance my mother had of hammering out a good bargain. Once purchased, these wonders were locked in my mother's parlour press until Christmas Eve, the big day of decorating.

Finally the day of the school holidays came, and we arrived home ecstatic with expectation. Now it was only a matter of days. The next step was 'bringing the Christmas'. My mother and father set out early one morning and headed into town on their own. There was usually one or two of us in tow when they went to town but not when they were 'bringing the Christmas.' It was an adult-only expedition.

The previous Saturday, the geese had been carried by pony and crib to the Christmas market, and as a result my mother had money in her pocket. She held back a number of geese, some of which she had plucked and made oven-ready for her town sister and cousins. My father took his favourite friend a bag of his best spuds.

Strangely enough, geese, and later turkeys, got posted – nationwide as well as overseas. I am not at all sure they always arrived in an edible condition. I can remember posting pounds of butter to England, which at the time seemed perfectly normal but would today be unthinkable.

We waited all day, bursting with excitement, until, as darkness fell, we heard the pony's hooves clip-clop down the boreen. We were allowed help carry in some of the boxes and put them on the parlour table. Others my mother insisted on carrying carefully herself. In the boxes were big barmbracks and seed loaves which the shops where we dealt gave as tokens of appreciation for our custom. Sometimes there was a home-made cake and pudding, made by our town aunt, or a wooden box full of black porter bottles from a cousin who had a pub in town. They were all put in a deep press to which my mother alone had the key. Christmas was now safely locked up in the parlour.

So presents did move around, but they were of a totally practical nature. Even Santa had a practical turn of mind, and I remember getting a new cardigan and jumper once and being absolutely delighted with them. Occasionally he did rise to dolls and wooden toys, which were cherished for years. Toys were as rare as hen's teeth, and when they did come they were a source of endless play.

Later, when I had my own children, buying 'Santa' brought me immense pleasure. The shrieks of joy on Christmas morning made all the mental scrutiny of deciding on the appropriate gift for each child worthwhile. Starting off with four boys, it was all about building blocks and model trains. When a girl finally arrived, I was delighted to be back into the world of dolls. For her first Christmas, Santa brought my daughter a beautiful doll and pram. They were both bigger than her, and our eldest, who was no longer a believer, informed me with amusement, 'You bought those for yourself, you know.' He was right.

Christmas shopping when you are a working wife with young children has to be a study in time and motion. When I was in that situation, helping to run our village shop and post office, Christmas was hectic.

So my Christmas shopping expedition had to be planned with military precision and usually executed in a one-day outing. Hence the need for a well-thought-out list.

On the morning of that special day, I hit town as soon as the shop doors opened. A child-free day to do the shops was a rare treat, and the challenge to get my list complete was a great stimulant. I began my campaign with pep in my step and began to tick off my acquisitions with immense satisfaction. The secret was to keep focused.

Before launching on a Christmas present safari, a shopping list has always been high on my agenda. With the belief that most money is hard-earned comes a conviction that if at all possible the spending of it should be sheer enjoyment. A list is the foundation stone of that enjoyment. One might not always adhere to the list, but it is like a road map or a satnav when setting out on a journey. Without some sense of direction, you could finish up going around in circles or, worse still, going nowhere. Worse again, you could end up in the wrong shops.

Making out a Christmas shopping list can be hugely enjoyable. I love it. It fills me with a great sense of anticipation. In the process, you may discover a few home truths about yourself as well. You begin with your nearest and dearest. Deciding what might give

BRENDAN KENNELLY

A Time for Voices

SELECTED POEMS 1960-1990

SEAMUS
HEANEY

them most joy can be a joy in itself. Then, gradually you work outwards until you find yourself with the guilty-conscience brigade: the 'duty' presents. As Shakespeare said, 'Conscience makes cowards of us all.' Conscience sometimes demands a high price, and you have to be very careful not to find yourself allocating these recipients more than they deserve. It could be to ease your conscience about your lack of warm feelings towards them. Chances are that this bad judgement overcomes you when drifting around the shops and you get caught up in the tide of the prevailing Christmas euphoria. A wave of goodwill to all your fellow humans suffuses you, including those who have been a bloody pain in the butt for the past year! This is when a list is a stalwart support because with it you have already overcome the guilt that causes bad decisions. Backwards psychology? Maybe. But tried and tested.

Sometimes when out Christmas shopping your eye can happen on an item that just hits the spot, and you think, *Wow, so-and-so would simply love that.* It may not be on your list, but it would be far more desirable than the original item. It is great when that happens. For other items, you simply have to trudge around relentlessly. Sometimes you might eventually strike oil, but other times you may simply have to change gear and think in a new direction.

When I begin to flag and feel that my decision-making capabilities are dwindling, I retire to a city-centre restaurant where I seek out a table in a quiet corner and review the situation over an enjoyable meal. The temptation of a glass of wine is resisted, as lunchtime wine and I do not lead to clear-headed decisions. This is a day for clear thinking.

Back in action, I forge ahead, and sometimes retrace my footsteps to reconsider an item previously rejected. Eventually I allow myself into a bookshop. One year, I made the mistake of beginning in a bookshop, and that was a disaster. Bookshops are great places for dawdling, and it was too early in the day for dawdling. It was like having the dessert before the main course. But by late afternoon, the bookshop is exactly what the doctor ordered. Having crossed off most of my list, it is time to head home where, when the children were small, 'Santa' was hastily bundled into an old wardrobe in Aunty Peg's spare room next door, the equivalent of my mother's parlour press.

In the very early years of my many Christmas shopping expeditions, I committed the unforgivable offence of putting myself before all of humankind. I decided that Christmas was all about joy to the world, and that that world included me. So I bought myself a present. And I have continued to do so every Christmas since. This way, you can be dead sure that you finish up with at least one present with which you are absolutely thrilled. That, for me, is always a book. One of my first self-indulgences in that field was a hardback copy of W. B. Yeats's poems. He was followed by Patrick Kavanagh, Brendan Kennelly, Ted Hughes, Billy Collins and others. These Christmas presents have enriched my life. And that is what Christmas is all about.

Christmas
Market

I t was to be a first for us, our very own Christmas market. Our local church was in dire need of restoration, and a Christmas craft fair might be the solution to our problem. The plan was that all the items for sale would be created by hand in the parish. Not one shop-bought item was to be displayed on our stalls. Did we have enough creativity amongst us to come up with goods of sufficient quality? Could we produce enough to provide the variety necessary for a really top-class market? Had we still got the skills to create beautiful things in our own homes?

A wonderful programme called *Hands*, filmed and produced by the far-seeing David Shaw-Smith in the 1970s, captured the craft skills being practised across the country. Watching an update programme in which some of the same craftspeople were interviewed was a sobering experience. Many of our crafts have been abandoned. Might we have 'sold our heritage for a mess of pottage'?

Lack of money can sometimes stimulate wonderful creativity. If money is readily available to throw at a problem, other possibilities may never be explored. When we Irish were less prosperous, we honed many skills. We baked, knitted, crocheted, sewed, grew our own food, wove and turned wood. When things were broken, we mended and recycled. These skills are now often abandoned for faster and seemingly more efficient solutions.

What appears in the short term to be making financial sense may in the long term prove to be not so desirable. Because when we bury our creativity, we lose our souls. Our creativity is the oil that eases the wheels of our minds, and an easy mind is necessary for our general well-being. We can pay a high price for putting financial experts in the driving seat. For them, money is the name of the game. One of my bright-brained young friends who is employed in a high-flying financial institution recently had to work over Christmas. 'Money never sleeps,' he explained.

Months before our planned Christmas market, the wheels were set in motion. Creating beautiful handmade things is not a speedy exercise, so time was necessary to give people the opportunity to get going on whatever they felt was their specific creative ability. In each one of us is a pool of creativity, and all around our parish these pools began to stir. People were enthused by the prospect of applying themselves to their chosen hobby or skill for the restoration of their church, which was no longer a thing of beauty – the passage of the years had taken its toll. Nothing stimulates the creative mind like a prospective project.

Lacemaking, crochet, patchwork, wood-turning, tapestry, carpentry, painting and knitting were discussed.
People exchanged knitting patterns or inquired if
there was a need for their wood-carving and carpentry skills.

Over the summer months we collected rose petals,
deadheading the roses in all the gardens to make potpourri. We laid the petals out on cotton sheets in the
gardens to be dried in the sun, then filled dozens of
wooden bowls – produced by one of our woodturners – with the sweet-smelling sun-dried rose petals.
Wrapped in cellophane and labelled 'Innishannon
Potpourri', they made lovely Christmas stocking fill-
ers. Their exquisite gold labels came from New York,
where a parishioner's daughter was excelling in the
world of luxury-goods presentation.

Next we decided to take on the waxy challenge
of Christmas candle-making. With very little experience we equipped ourselves with a glossy book on the
art of candle-making as well as with moulds, stearin
powder and the other paraphernalia needed for the
job. The keys to our success were the big balls of pure
beeswax that were stored in an old trunk in the attic –
the product of years of beekeeping by my cousin Con,
who had kept hives in the back garden.

We put Aunty Peg's old heavy preserving pot on
the Aga and into it landed the lumps of beeswax. They

slowly softened as we gently circled them around the pot with a large wooden spoon. Gradually the wax melted, and as it began to diminish the pot filled with a dark, rich, golden liquid. With this we had the basic ingredient for our pure wax candles. Having added the other requirements to the pot, we put a taper into a candle mould and carefully poured in liquid wax, endeavouring to keep the wick at the centre. Then we allowed the liquid to rest and the air bubbles to escape. When the wax had settled, we filled in the little well that had formed to give the candle a level base.

The more candles we made, the more we learnt about the process. Instead of standing the mould in water to cool before the removal of the candle, as the book instructed, we found that putting it in the fridge for a few minutes was more effective and less messy. We also discovered that placing the mould in the freezer for a few minutes helped with the ejection of the candle. The more we made the easier the process became, and we finished up with about fifty satin-smooth candles, all smelling of pure honey. These we stood into solid wooden candlesticks created by our woodturners. They looked good and made lovely Christmas gifts, especially for someone living far from Innishannon.

Through spring, summer and autumn there were rumours of many hands at work throughout the

parish, but it was difficult to know just how many until we let it be known that it was time to bring in the harvest. Bags and boxes of amazing workmanship began to come in. Because our house is big and rambling and in the centre of the village, it was decided to make this the collection depot. Having everything at the one location would make it easier to ascertain what exactly we had for our Christmas market.

First the return came in a trickle that turned into a steady flow and then finished up in a tidal wave. Bags and boxes filled the large front room, the smaller *seomra ciúin* and all along the long winding hallway. It was truly amazing. Beautiful lace christening outfits, patchwork quilts, exquisite tapestry pictures, handcrafted lamps, paintings and even little perfectly made tables. Another day, a full box of beautifully created Christmas stockings with two hand-stitched patchwork cot quilts was handed in. With every new arrival our wonder grew. We were truly gobsmacked. The return was beyond all expectations. When we thought that we had seen it all and that the standard could not get any higher, something else would arrive to take our breath away.

Two items in particular were amazing, both gorgeous tapestry pictures. One was of an elegant wine bottle surrounded by delicately coloured fruit. It was the work of a woman who had created beautiful tapestry designs all her life and had made it a fine art. How could you put a price on such beauty? This gentle lady was not even a member of the church she was supporting. Everybody who saw the picture gasped in delight, and one woman declared that she was going to buy it, no matter what price went on it. And she did.

The second one was a tapestry of a bowl of exquisite roses woven by an English lady who had recently moved into the parish and who was intrigued by the whole concept of a local Christmas market. When another lady with an eye for a beautiful creation saw this picture, she decided to get her six children who were all going to buy her individual Christmas presents to pool their resources and buy it for her.

It was difficult to believe that all these high-quality goods could come out of one small parish. The standard was unbelievable. When publicising our Christmas market, we let it be known that this was not to be a bargain-basement sale but an opportunity to get one-off rare items, probably the family heirlooms of the future. When one local heard this, she caustically commented, 'No bargains to be had there.' She was right. People had put such time and effort into creating all these beautiful things, and we did not want to demean this workmanship by selling them off cheaply. After all, these goods had not poured off an anonymous

non-stop assembly line. Their creators had put many hours of exacting precision and love into them. They deserved good homes where they would be loved, cared for and appreciated.

At last we were ready to roll. The plan was that our Christmas market would be held in the function room of our local Innishannon Hotel, a wonderful venue beside the village, on the banks of the river Bandon. The fair would run for Saturday and Sunday on a weekend before Christmas when people were in the mood for shopping.

The stalls really should have been set up on the Friday evening, but this was not possible as the hotel had a wedding that day, so the transport of our goods had to be put on hold until the early hours of Saturday morning after the revellers had finally gone to bed. We had a blueprint ready, with all our craft items sorted into different categories and a proposed layout plan, and we knew in advance the exact plan of campaign once the function room was available.

At 4am on Saturday morning, we loaded up two large vans provided by our local garage and set out for the hotel. It was a crisp, dry, frosty morning, and when we arrived the hotel staff were on hand to whip long tables into place. Like clockwork, the plan went into action, and we laid out our stalls. When all the beautiful things were displayed, they were breathtaking.

Tables groaned with homemade Christmas cakes and all kinds of seasonal eats. Oil paintings were standing on easels, lace christening gowns were displayed on large dolls, tables gleamed with glowing woodwork, and all kinds of handcrafted goods were laid along counters. There was a collective glow of pride and satisfaction that our parish had produced all of this.

The doors were thrown open at 10am, and people poured in. Our Christmas market had been well heralded in the local press, and people came sensing that this was an opportunity to purchase a gift to remember. There was no time for long pondering as a more decisive purchaser might make a move while you were dithering. This happened to one man who was impressed by a hand-knit Nativity scene into which one good knitter had put many hours of dedication. He decided to have a stroll around the other stalls to see if better value was available only to witness his crib sailing out the door in the arms of an alert teacher. She wanted it for her young students and knew a good thing when she saw it.

As is always the case, the early birds got the most beautiful things. A lot of the craftspeople were manning the stalls, and they got immense satisfaction to see their handiwork receive such appreciation. All the craftspeople, both stallholders and customers, enjoyed the opportunity to discuss their skills and techniques.

As it was a dry, crisp day, people were delighted to walk along the riverside and meander into the hotel dining room for lunch or tea and then to come back into the fair for another browse.

By the end of the second day, our counters were bare. We were all exhausted but glowing with satisfaction. Our Christmas market had been a glorious triumphant finale to a year during which a pool of parish creativity had swirled into motion and a profusion of perfect presents had emerged that had enriched the spirits of the creators and provided many beautiful things to give delight and joy for generations.

Open House

The late autumn leaves crunch beneath our feet as we make our way under the overhanging trees along the narrow road towards Bride Park Cottage. We are on our annual pilgrimage to DJ Murphy's open house. DJ, who owns Bandon Garden Centre, is a man of many artistic talents. At Christmas, he turns his beautiful period home into a Christmas masterpiece and opens his house and gardens to the public to raise money for charity. Every year it is different, and every year breathtaking. We come here to see, smell, feel and get the flavour of Christmas.

Turning at the stone-pillared gateway, the garden stretches out around us into wooded contours. The curving avenue is a mysterious walk through lit trees that dilute the dusk to reveal tall tree ferns fanning their fronds like dark swans and creamy white hellebores gleaming shyly from beneath their canopied leaves. Amongst them, cloaked ladies and top-hatted gentlemen view us from a distance. This is a world of mystery, imagery and make-believe, a winter wonderland.

Coming around the last curve of the avenue, the narrow windows of the gabled house come into view, and Christmas candles glow behind frosted windowpanes. Here, in 1828, was born Patrick Ronayne

Cleburne, who became a Confederate major general in the American Civil War, which makes this house a place of pilgrimage for American historians. It is a quaint, quirky, atmospheric house of narrow corridors and cavernous fireplaces, which DJ, a collector of beautiful things, has furnished with period pieces.

Our footsteps resound off the old quarry-tiled floor of the small front porch where stained-glass windows are muted by candlelight. The opening of the door into the main house emits a gush of warm aromatic air, and from rooms at both ends of the long corridor we glimpse glowing log fires. We are drawn into a room of Victorian opulence where an enormous overmantel mirror above a glowing log fire reflects a sparkling chandelier of cut crystal edged with gold. Gilt-framed portraits of beautiful ladies with ample cleavages and military garbed gentlemen adorn the walls.

The atmosphere breathes the slower pace of another era, and we need meandering time to better absorb all the minute attention to detail. On top of a baby grand piano spellbinding Christmas scenes bring us to a standstill, and in a deep bay-window recess is a ceiling-high Christmas tree, its glowing lights reflected in the window behind it. Beyond this, a door opens into a glass-domed room where Christmas floral arrangements overflow off elegant stands and realistic-looking white bears and reindeers peer down

from equally realistic-looking snow-covered hills.

Along the hallway, in a candlelit room, a long table is laid out for fine dining, with gorgeous embroidered napery and crested embossed tableware. Sideboards are laden with Christmas fare and candelabra. Everywhere frosted windows glow with candles and richly detailed enchanting decorations. Log fires crackle, and comfortable red plush chairs invite you to sit a while and enjoy this old-world festive season. Elegant chaises longues evoke images of reclining ladies.

Appreciative visitors exchange their impressions in hushed voices, pointing out their preferences to each other, wanting their friends and, indeed, total strangers to enjoy every tiny detail. To miss anything would be to skip a vital page in this book of Christmas Past. We drift along a dimly lit narrow corridor, where the walls invite us to linger, to enjoy and be entertained by a range of fascinating pictures.

Coming to the end of the corridor, we reluctantly push open a heavy wooden door and suddenly are enveloped into a blaze of brilliant light in an enormous, warm, welcoming kitchen, buzzing with talk, tea, mulled wine and mince pies. This large kitchen, with its laden dressers and tables of festive fare smelling of cinnamon and spices, is the throbbing heart of the house. Since this open house is an annual fundraiser for a local charity, volunteers make, bake and serve Christmas fare, all to be enjoyed in comfortable commodious chairs and soft reclining sofas around a huge log fire. Old friends meet up, and there is much laughter and fun as people discuss the different aspects of the house and their Christmas plans and wish each other the compliments of the season.

We are reluctant to leave this heady warmth and step out into the chilly air outside, but the beaming windows of the old coach house across the yard entice us out. Christmas angels and sparkling stars twinkle on the trees and lead us to the door of the old stone building. On the way we are tempted by the perfect Christmas plants and rows of rich red Poinsettias. Suddenly, strains of music come from under the surrounding trees, and young carol singers emerge, red-hatted and warm-coated, filling the air with 'Silent Night'. Cold forgotten, we stand and savour the moment.

Finally we make it to the arched oak door and into the high-raftered barn, where a huge open fire surrounded by ancient cooking pots sends out warmth. This converted coach house is tonight a Christmas wonderland, selling a variety of magical decorations. The problem here is what *not* to buy. DJ has an eye for the perfect Christmas decoration, and, despite strong resistance, we come out laden with bags of 'must-haves'. But this is Christmas, and even Ebeneezer Scrooge would be unable to resist Bride Park Cottage.

The Christmas
Press

SEASONS GREETINGS

NEWBRIDGE
silverware

better

Trees

Balls

res

mes better

During the months of spring, summer, autumn and into early winter, Christmas sleeps in an old press along the hallway behind my kitchen. On the top shelf of this press are two long boxes, each containing a regal-looking Santa Claus, both of whom became surplus to requirement in our local shop when a more modern decorating scheme was introduced. Rather than permit them to face the ignominy of unemployment and an early skip demise, I adopted them, and, over the years, they have shown their appreciation. Every Christmas they take up guard duty along the hallway in their red cloaks and impressive staffs, where they keep a look out for intruders.

Living with these two venerable aristocrats is a large, florid, flamboyant Santa, a present from a sister who believes that Christmas should be celebrated with bling and outrageous exuberance. He sports a shimmering gold jacket and trousers stretched beyond their capabilities over his huge pot belly. A rakish hat is worn at a jaunty angle over a pair of roguish eyes that dance with merriment. He is the picture of bad taste and debauchery, Christmas bling at its worst, but he brings an instant smile to your face. Come Christmas, this Santa jumps onto the top of the kitchen press.

From his lofty domain he smiles roguishly down over all the goings-on below. A certain distance is required from his overpowering presence so this high perch slightly diminishes his garish glow.

Stuffed between these three large guys at the top of the Christmas press is a tattered flexible snowman made more so by years of being pushed into tight corners. His snowy brilliance has diminished to grey slush, and he is not far from a final meltdown. On the next shelf comes the first priority of my Christmas decorating: the crib. It is better to be more specific and say: the main crib. Because I have five cribs. Too many, you are probably thinking and I agree, but, you see, they are not here by design but rather by the way things have evolved.

The main crib is the one I bought for my first Christmas in Innishannon in 1961. It has seen me through many Christmases and is a little bit the worse for wear. When Aunty Peg and Uncle Jacky died, I inherited their crib, so the two became one. These two cribs have absorbed a miscellaneous collection of other adoptions, which, packed into a retired banana box, find their way onto the credenza at the end of the hall at Christmas.

Once, on a visit to Sligo, I happened into what looked like a butcher's shop but was in fact the shop of a master woodcarver, Michael Quirke, who had

turned from being a butcher into a woodworker. I brought home one crib figure, and later the rest of the family followed. This weighty wooden crib goes on the window of the *seomra ciúin*, where it can be viewed by children passing by on the street outside.

Then, out of the blue, another crib came into our house. When my daughter turned eighteen, her aunt decided to present her with a crib which I had bought for the home farm with my first wage packet. It cost the princely sum of seventeen shillings and sixpence – which may sound like a pittance, but my wages at the time were just two pounds and ten shillings so it was almost one-third of my wages. Unbelievably, after all those years it was still intact and even came wrapped up in the original box.

When it arrived back to me, years later, I looked at it in open-mouthed wonder and was quite chuffed that my sister had cared for it so lovingly. It is still with me as my daughter has young children and feels that it is safer here. So that is crib number three. This goes on top of the television press. (My television, when silent, lives behind the closed doors of a press.) This is an ideal location for this little china crib.

Crib number four is not really a crib but the stable of a crib made by a son when he was in a woodwork class in school. It has no figures, but come Christmas I place in it a large baby Jesus moulded for me

many years ago by Sr Eithne who once taught me in Drishane convent. Years later, she came to live in our parish in St Patrick's, Upton, where she helped to care for the residents with special needs. I was particularly fond of this nun as she taught me many things that in later life proved invaluable. So her baby Jesus is special. This treasured crib, with its special Jesus, goes beneath the tree.

There is yet another, tiny, crib, which was a gift from a dear friend. It has to be stored in a tin box due to its fragility as it is actually made out of wood shavings. And it has to be very carefully situated as it has a tendency to topple over. It usually rests on a cut-crystal cake stand on top of Aunty Peg's sideboard, where its delicacy is reflected in the glass. All the cribs, packed carefully into retired banana boxes, take up a full section of my Christmas press.

Another is missing – a little cardboard crib bought for two shillings many years ago when we were children. Because of its delicacy, it was stored away very carefully. So carefully that I cannot now remember where.

On the shelves beneath the cribs are the boxes for the different areas of the house. There is the Christmas tree box containing the lights and many smaller boxes of baubles and miscellaneous odds and ends for the tree. There is the *seomra ciúin* box, with the overmantel decorations, including a string of little multicoloured presents bought many years ago on a Christmas shopping expedition with my sister. Then there is the front hall box, the kitchen box and the front room box. There is the box of cloths, including a richly embossed banner of the Holy Family created by people in the Cope Foundation which graces the inside of the front door. Finally, there is a huge, richly embroidered teddy bear dressed as Santa, made years ago by the residents of St Patrick's, Upton, under the guidance of Sr Attracta who ran a workshop there. Those residents and the nuns are now gone, but I am glad to have a sample of their craftsmanship. All these boxes wait in this old press, but come Christmas the doors will open and they will march out and find their way, like emigrants returning to their own corners all around the house.

Decorating
the House

My grandmother, who held very traditional views, was not overly enthusiastic about Christmas trees, declaring them to be of foreign origin. She informed us that they were not rooted in our Gaelic culture and so were not to be part of her Christmas ritual. Instead, she placed her tall, white Christmas candle on the window and edged her windowpanes with holly and ivy leaves that transformed her Christmas window into something magical.

As a result, my mother was not reared with the Christmas tree tradition, and when I was very young we did not have a Christmas tree in our house either. Nor did any of our neighbours. We dragged bundles of holly from the local wood and peeled strings of trailing ivy off the old trees in the fort and groves around the house. With all this greenery we decorated the kitchen. Ivy trailed from the meat hooks on the ceiling. Holly was poked behind every picture – more with enthusiasm than artistry.

My mother dispatched us with bundles of holly to any neighbouring house where there were no children to do the collecting and the dragging home across the fields. The big pay-off for doing these deliveries was that our elderly neighbours were happy to let us do the decorating, and we were even happier as we got a free run decorating a house with no competing sisters.

One Christmas, my eldest sister decided to fill the gap in our festive requirements. She went on the prowl around the farm for a suitable tree to meet her needs. This brought her into conflict with my father, who was a planter but not a feller of trees. After many arguments, during which we backed up our pioneering sister and heard our father's usual prayer of 'God pity the man who has five daughters', he yielded to female pressure. A compromise was reached, and a settlement agreed on a large branch of a pine tree he had planted as a young man. He insisted on cutting the branch himself as he did not want one of his trees permanently disfigured by his marauding daughters. He listened to but did not follow instructions as to the height and width of the requested branch.

This Christmas branch masquerading as a tree stood on the kitchen's second table, which catered for the overflow of activities from the main table. Usually an enamel bucket of spring water stood here and another of fresh milk filled daily for household needs. It also served as a desk for our homework and a base for my mother's sewing machine when it came into action. Over Christmas, however, all such activities were suspended, and it became the home for our gramophone, which normally resided in the parlour – and, now, it also held the tree, or branch.

The Christmas branch did not have the required balance to stand independently and needed to have its back to the wall to keep it upright. So it leant against the wall beside the clock, which had my father in a constant state of red alert in case it took a sideways slide and upset the balance of the clock about which he was unbelievably paranoid. My father daily monitored this clock's precision by Greenwich Mean Time on the BBC, not trusting the inexperienced Raidió Éireann for reliability. One would assume that once the tree was decorated his clock would be out of danger, but this was not the case. His daughters' Christmas tree decorating was a work in progress, and the job was never quite finished to our satisfaction. The fact that the tree decorations were simply balloons and Christmas cards did nothing to dampen our enthusiasm. Fairy lights had yet to twinkle in rural Ireland, and the only fairies we had heard of lived in the fairy fort behind our house. With us five sisters, it was a case of 'anything you can do, I can do better'. When tinsel eventually made it into our world, it brightened up our Christmas tree, which by then had become a real tree and had made it down onto the floor, fitting comfortably into a corner under the sloping stairs.

The crib, strangely enough, featured very little in

our home's decoration, apart from a little cardboard model, the purchase of which had seriously stretched our financial resources. All the emphasis was on the life-size model at the back of the church. But with sheep out on the hills and other animals nearby in the stable and stalls, it was easy to imagine that the living crib of Bethlehem was all around us.

When I arrived in Innishannon, I never had to go in search of a Christmas tree. Charlie, who delivered the post, threw the gift of a tree in over our garden wall the week before Christmas. This went on for many years until my generous neighbour went on to real Christmas land in the heavens. For a few years after that I went to the garden centre for my tree until a local farmer, John, decided to diversify into Christmas trees.

Every year in early December his extensive farm-yard fills up with a huge variety of trees with which he supplies the whole parish. It is a case of come early if you want to have the best selection. I love choos-ing the Christmas tree, and John and his helpers have endless patience in dragging out trees from the rows and waltzing them around the yard so that they can be viewed from all angles. As I am a bit of a dith-erer, it takes me ages to reach a decision, but they pull out all the stops to send me home happy. Then they deliver the tree at a time of my choosing and erect it in the usual corner of the front room after it has been trimmed to fit snugly, with its trunk standing in a basin of water to prevent dehydration. It stands tall and elegant between two windows, waiting to be decorated for Christmas.

One would imagine that when decorating a house for Christmas one would start in the front hallway. It is the obvious place from where to take off. But no. I begin in the middle of the house in the *seomra ciúin*. Maybe it is because the *seomra ciúin* is the winter room of the home. Once the fire is lit in there it is the heart of the house, and Christmas is at the heart of winter.

Getting through winter would be a very difficult voyage but for Christmas. It is the glow in the middle of this cold bleak season that keeps us all going through grey, chilly, barren days. We focus on Christmas, and, like a lighthouse, it guides us on through choppy waters and brings light into the darkness. Ecclesiastes is wise when it states that there is a season for everything – and winter is definitely the season for Christmas. It is probably why even people who do not believe in the Christmas story get caught up in the magic. We need a reason to forget about the cold outside and toast our toes at the fire.

In the *seomra ciúin*, the fireplace is the starting point. The overmantel is a great structure on which to hang Christmas decorations. Before the draping begins,

holly branches are laid along the top, and, if the branches fall correctly they extend out along over the frames of the two portraits on either side. These are portraits of the two Lenas, grandmother and grand-daughter, painted by local artist Jerry Larkin. It was Lena Senior who engendered a love of Christmas in all her tribe.

Now for the string of tiny brightly coloured boxes that twine up and down through the various tiny shelves and curves of the overmantel. Then on go waxed wreaths bought so long ago that I forget where. These are the only constant performers as all the other bits and pieces get put wherever the fancy takes. Usually two fat Santas strut their stuff on the small shelves, and gradually all the other candidates find a home. There is much twigging and tweaking until satisfaction is reached. If you enjoy painting or flower arranging, the chances are that you enjoy Christmas decorating.

Around the room, holly is edged along the tops of the pictures, with particular attention paid to the painting of my old home that hangs on the wall over a desk, right opposite the door. This old roll-top desk was bought years ago in a junk shop wearing a coat of black peeling paint. When, with blood, sweat and tears, the dreadful coat was eased off, there was a body of warm honey-coloured oak underneath. It has served me faithfully for years – first as a base for doing accounts but in more recent times for the more enjoyable pursuit of letter-writing. Yes, I am one of those antiques who still write letters.

In the painting above the desk I tried to capture the ambience of the home house in oils, and now this painting brings my old home into the room. It is not a masterpiece, but it was painted with love. In the same shop where I found the desk was an old gilt frame that fitted this picture like a glove.

Different little Christmas mementoes find their way onto the top of the desk and along bookshelves around the room until I am left with an empty box. All that remains to be done in this room is the wooden crib for the window, but that is a job for closer to Christmas.

Next on the agenda is the front hall. Another bundle of holly from the back porch is landed centre stage, and two more boxes from the Christmas press are brought forth. Out of the boxes containing the Christmas cloths comes the colourful banner of the Holy Family. This goes on the back of the front door, which has been its location every Christmas since it was given to me, about twelve years ago, by my niece Eileen. She bought it at a Christmas market held as a fund-raiser for the Cope Foundation.

The two small tables in the hall are covered with

rich red tablecloths. A bit over the top? Definitely. But you can get away with all that at Christmas. On these tables go well-loved Christmas mementoes. My favourite is a little carol singer in a brown velvet cloak straight out of a Victorian Christmas card. Here standing against the wall is a large ornately framed mirror which slipped from its mooring on the wall above a few years ago and landed unharmed on the floor. Before I had decided to rehang it more securely, one of my friends, who considers herself more knowledgeable then me in interior design, advised leaving it on the floor. Apparently that is now quite acceptable in design circles. As Michelangelo once said, 'I am still learning.'

Along the hallway the pictures all get a thatch of holly and red ribbon with the odd robin perching amongst them. A detour into the kitchen, where the dressers invite decorating, and the Christmas cards draped along the top display varied Christmas scenes – above them all is a thatch of red berry holly. Once in a craft shop I picked up a string of tiny clothes pegs which are perfect Christmas card holders and ideal for the shutters of the window. The glitzy Santa looking like an overweight cheerleader beams down at me from the top of the kitchen press. Then out into the back porch with the denuded holly branches. They get a quick pruning into a basket and are taken to the *seomra ciúin*, where they will make good fire starters. A quick whip around the house to gather up the empty boxes and back into the Christmas press with them.

By then I am beginning to creak at the seams, but stickatitness clocks in, and out comes the Hoover for a quick swish around the floors. *Stickatitness* is a word not found in any dictionary. It was coined by the old nun who ran the school laundry. While demonstrating the art of ironing, she proclaimed that the success of any job was down to sticking with the project on hand. All done, I put on the kettle and collapse on to the kitchen couch.

Moss Gathering

L ate on a Sunday evening before Christmas
when the light is fading, I head into Dromkeen wood with a canvas bag under my arm. For
some reason I do not want anybody to see me in
the wood filling my bag with moss. Maybe I have a
hidden fear that there is now an EU directive forbid-
ding such activities.

Dromkeen wood sprawls along a hill overlook-
ing our village. I can see it from my front windows,
and its trees announce the comings and goings of
the seasons. A slight veil of vivid green foretells the
coming of spring. It slowly deepens into the varied
hues of summer and then matures into Technicolor
in autumn. That, in turn, fades into the dull greys and
browns of winter. Every season the wood brings its
own magic.

Over the years I have walked its paths and climbed
its slopes in all seasons just for the sheer joy of it, but
this December I go there for a lowly reason, to raid
its wooded inclines for moss. There is something mysterious about Dromkeen wood in the fading light.
Bushes take on odd shapes, and between the shadowy
tree trunks you catch glimpses of the dark river in the
valley below. The river reflects the Old Tower and the

steeples of Christ Church and St Mary's on the hill across the valley.

As I walk along the path, squelching layers of faded leaves beneath my feet, my hand searches the high bracken-covered bank beside me. Most of the ferns have given up their struggle to withstand the sodden conditions and have folded their fronds into winter sleep. But beneath and around them the moss thrives in the prevailing moist conditions. With my seeking hand I determine its depths, sensing by touch if it is deep or just skimpily covering the bank. Where it is deep and moist, I ease it gently in large soft clumps away from the bank and slip it into my bag. Some fallen tree trunks are covered in deep blankets of moss that peel back easily.

By now my bag is bulging with large, soft rolls of moss, but still as light as a feather. Now I am deep into the wood, and darkness is creeping in through the trees so it is time to head for home with my stolen goods. Nature is bountiful, and having a wood close by is a great source of richness for all of us. As I clamber down the steep meandering paths, I catch a glimpse of the brightly coloured fairy doors that provide such wonderment for the children. In front of some of the doors are little notes left for the fairies, and over Christmas many of the children will come here to visit them.

Back home, I am anxious to unroll the moss to test its ability to cover the crib. This is to be the first year using moss – up until now I have always used straw. I got the moss idea a week ago on a pre-Christmas visit to Hayfield Manor, a hotel where they take their Christmas decorating seriously. They had incorporated moss very effectively in their impressive foyer crib. Visits to posh hotels are not only about enjoying the good food and the ambience but also about bringing home their smart ideas.

The location for my principal crib is on a credenza at the end of the front hall. I acquired this credenza many years ago in a junk shop, which may or may not have been an antique shop. Sometimes it is difficult to be quite sure whether you are in a junk shop or an antique shop. Maybe the prices are a clue – you have a better chance of a bargain in a junk shop. Searching through the debris is half the enjoyment. I came upon this little mahogany press fronted by two mirrored doors, with a marble top reflected in a mirrored back. It was a pretty unusual piece, and I had no idea what it was. When I inquired, I was told, 'That is a credenza.'

'What is a credenza?' I asked, puzzled.

'Well, in earlier days, when the nobility dined, there was the possibility that they could be poisoned by their enemies in league with their own servants. So in order to make sure that the food was uncontaminated before going to table, it was first placed on a credenza, and a servant tasted it to make sure that it was safe to eat.'

It's amazing what you learn in a junk shop. To be a servant in those days, you had to prove your credentials in more ways than one. After a certain amount of price negotiation, and without tasting a bite, I became the proud owner of the credenza. It moved into my hallway, where it turned into the storage cupboard and, once a year, the foundation for the crib. A far cry from aristocratic dining but retaining royal connotations at the same time.

The stable for my crib is a large, amazingly shaped piece of bleached driftwood retrieved many years ago from the beach in Ballybunion, Co. Kerry. Its intriguing shape caught my eye, and we dragged it for miles along the beach. Saturated with seawater it was a dead weight, but, fascinated by its potential, I pulled it along determinedly, much to my children's annoyance. It was years before they appreciated its beauty. It spends the summer in the garden and then comes in for Christmas to be a fitting home for the Nativity scene. It has the appearance of an arched cave with stalagmites shooting skywards. One of the stalagmites is the ideal bearer for the star.

The piece of driftwood is heavy and cumbersome. I am put to the pin of my collar to effect a safe land-

ing on top of the credenza, but with a lot of huffing and puffing the end is achieved. Then there is a bit of balancing and levelling to achieve secure positioning. Mary and Joseph had enough problems on their holy heads not to mind having the roof collapse in on top of them in the midst of proceedings.

Stable secure, it is time for the moss to unfold. It comes out of the bag in soft deep rolls like top-quality carpet and covers the floor of the stable. Then out into the stable yard and up onto the roof and over the surrounding mountains. The moss is magical and transforms the credenza top and driftwood into my vision of Bethlehem. The white peaks of the ancient driftwood shoot high above the mounds of moss like snow-covered mountains above a lush green valley.

This ancient driftwood, which was heaved from the depths of the ocean, breathes antiquity. The water in its rolling depths moulded its contours and then cast it ashore. Now it has found a new location to tell a story rooted in time. The moss brings with it the stillness of quiet woodlands. The crib holds a hush of expectancy. It is ready for its royal visitors.

On the wall above the crib hangs a painting of an old stone cow house from the home farm. With its rusty galvanised door and narrow slit windows, it comes from an earlier farming world. I always loved that old stall and had really enjoyed putting it on canvas. When it was completed, Br Albert, a patient saint of a man who had tried to make an artist out of me, looked at the picture. 'You did a good job there,' he told me.

'Just loved that old stall,' I told him.

'Always shows in a painting,' he smiled.

The picture and the crib tell the story of another time. The box containing the rest of the story is on the floor in front of the credenza. It is time to tell it. I love this story, it has a magic all of its own. As each piece emerges from the box it brings with it its own memories, and they all blend together to weave the magic of Christmas Past into the magic of Christmas Present. First out of the box come Mary and Joseph, who are older than myself, having been inherited from Aunty Peg. They are a bit battered by time. I have a little bit of a dilemma as there is a second Holy Family, this one bought on my first Christmas in Innishannon and a little bit less battered than the other. However, out of deference to seniority, Aunty Peg's gets pride of place. The second Joseph becomes a shepherd, because his garb is similar, and the second Mary becomes a *doula*, which is highly desirable with any new baby.

Mary and Joseph settle down in comfortable togetherness into the moss with baby Jesus between them. Then come two cows, two donkeys and a flock of sheep to breathe warmth on the little family. Next comes a group of shepherds – one of them missing a leg, the result of being over-loved down through the years by overly enthusiastic little admirers. He has to be strategically placed and fits into a curve in the driftwood against which he can lean for support. We have a lot in common.

Then comes a flock of geese. I saw them in a craft shop many years ago, and, because geese are synonymous to me with my mother and Christmas, I brought them home with me. Then come birds of all shapes and sizes. They nestle in the moss and perch on the uprights of the driftwood. A large flock of them have been collected over the years and others have been gifted by friends and family. Two white doves settle over the crib on the branches of the driftwood.

The original crib was all about bringing peace – and maybe the family that the heavenly choirs heralded but the human world rejected was warmly welcomed by the natural world. Then come more animals, angels and a miscellaneous collection of waifs and strays. As I take each piece out of its wrapping, I remember the buying or the gifting of it. Little carved angels bought in Germany, Venetian glass birds brought from Italy by an old priest relative, now long gone. The little drummer boy given by my mother.

When they are all in place, it is time for the star – a tricky business this as the star has a mind of its own

and wants to become a tilting star – or, worse still, a falling star. At last it is pinned on the highest peak of the driftwood with a white angel waving up at it from a lower peak. This is a special angel as she was crocheted for me by a dear friend to whom life had not been kind but who, nevertheless, spread kindness around her.

Then comes St Francis, whom I bore home under my arm from Assisi many years ago. Normally he resides in the garden, but come Christmas he takes up his position in front of the crib. It was this peaceful bird-loving man who first introduced the idea of erecting a crib at Christmastime to celebrate the first Christmas.

Now for the delicate business of lighting. This is my first year to have a properly lighted crib. At least, that is the plan. As this corner of the hall is not well lit, I had expressed a desire for light in the crib. An electrically minded son installed the required plug and provided the lights when he was home on holidays, assuring me that the whole procedure was foolproof.

I am not an electrical genius and am always amazed when my efforts are rewarded with success. I gingerly laid the fragile strings of lights strategically and hopefully artistically around my wildlife crib, entwining the little star, the angels' wings and the animals on the tops of the mountains. Then into the depths of the stable, giving the most light around the central figures so that the greatest glow was around the baby. The plan was to have the plug end finishing up at the power point, and, to my surprise, it did. Then for the big switching on. Would the whole thing light up? It did! My first properly lit crib. Joy to the world!

Waiting patiently until the crib is done, the Christmas tree stands in a pool of dark green foliage in the corner between two windows of the front room. This room links the kitchen to the front hallway and so is a bit of a commuter belt, with windows looking onto the village street. Sitting in here you can watch the world go by outside the window, and my husband very appropriately christened it the curiosity room. During the summer months, bumper-to-bumper traffic passes by into West Cork, and at Christmas, when the lights on our village tree across the road are turned on and the other trees along the street are festooned with fairy lights, they all dance together in a shimmer of festive glow.

From the Christmas press come the boxes of tree decorations, to be landed at the base of the tree. First the lights. While with the crib the lights are the finishing touch, with the tree they are the first step. Three long lengths of fairy lights wound carefully around cardboard are unwound and laid out along the floor for a test run. When they are plugged in and each one sparkles along the floor, there is a sigh of relief.

A stepladder is brought into action to reach the very top of the tree and drape the lights from there down along the branches. Bearing in mind the advice of my cautious neighbour that 'no one over sixty should mount a stepladder', I step on it with due care. I have no intention of giving him the satisfaction of telling me, 'I told you so.' The lights are guided down along the branches, blending in and out through the greenery, until the whole tree is entwined. Then another light test. They glow. I turn off the power to avoid any accidents while decorating. My pessimistic neighbour would have 'I told you so' ammunition for months.

First to land, on top of the tree, is the fairy queen, wearing a golden crown and flaunting a flowing, rich red, regal gown. Created for me by a friend who is gifted at lacemaking and crochet, this lady in red is queen of the Christmas tree. The first attempted landing by Her Royal Highness fails because there is not enough space between the peak of the tree and the ceiling to allow her to stand erect and display her finery to advantage. Down off the stepladder. After a search of the back porch, my small pruner is located, then back up the ladder and the top branch comes down a notch. Up goes Her Highness onto the trimmed peak, which disappears up under her flowing finery and holds her firmly in place. From her exalted location she can view her kingdom – she has the best view in the house.

The desired theme is red and gold, but unfortunately this decorator is not an observer of hard and fast rules so, as the decorating progresses, other hues filter in. A determined start is made with red, or at least mostly red, baubles, starting with miniatures at the top, growing in girth as they descend. Some have been around for a long time and are showing the dents of age. They have to be hung with the best side out. Others, acquired later at various Christmas shows, glow with newness and look good from any angle. Paper clips are slipped into hooks at the top to better allow dangling space. It is lovely to see all the baubles shimmering between the branches.

Finally the bauble boxes are empty, and the green tree has a red glow. Next the box containing delicate little golden trees, sleighs and angels is opened. These came from Germany, where the Christmas tree originated and where people are still masters of Christmas tree decorations. These are so light and petite that it is only when they catch the light that they shimmer and become visible, so hanging them at the right angle is a challenge. But when they glow they instantly make all the painstaking effort worthwhile.

Then sentiment comes into play, and on goes a fat, white hand-knitted snowman, bought at a Christmas fair by an appreciative sister who never cast on a knitting stitch in her life but who is hugely impressed by anyone who does. Then a small red purse, given as a gift many years ago to a little girl who became inordinately attached to it and who smiles in remembrance every Christmas when she sees it on the tree. Little Christmas stockings belonging to a beloved sister who lived in Canada but who always came home for Christmas. She adored Christmas and now is remembered on the tree. Three hand-knitted Santas, sent from America by a lady confined to a wheelchair who found the therapy of knitting soothing. A time-battered old Santa boot that has seen many Christmases and has the appearance of it.

And on it goes. Every decoration that comes out of the boxes has its own story, and the decorating of the tree is a journey over the years and to many parts of the world. It has the richness of remembering. Finally every little trinket has found a home, and the empty boxes go back into the Christmas press to await the return of their contents at a later date. The tree is overladen, overcrowded and full of remembrances. Next, it is down to ground level, where the tree's trunk is held firmly in place by an iron base. Beneath it is a basin of water to prevent dehydration. A red tablecloth is swirled around the base, hiding these unsightly objects. The wooden stable made by a young enthusiastic

carpenter, now no longer so young, goes under the tree, and into that the large baby Jesus moulded by Sr Eithne. It is lighting-up time, and the whole tree comes alive. Time to stand back and admire. Christmas is moving in.

With the tree done, it is time to tackle the surrounding room. The little china crib that I bought with my first pay packet goes on top of the television cupboard. Above this press is a painting of geese, which, over the years, has brought me hours of pleasant viewing – far more than the television beneath it.

My husband and I bought this painting in a West Cork gallery on our thirtieth wedding anniversary. We were out for the day and called into an art gallery on the way home. Amongst the other paintings was this one by Susan Webb of geese in a river surrounded by hills. I can still remember the first time I saw this picture. I was climbing up the stairs of the Old Mill Gallery in West Cork and the picture was strategically placed right at the top. It brought me to a standstill. I was back on the riverbank in our farm, watching the geese exulting in the flowing water. It was immediately obvious that this artist knew her geese. Geese have an odd way of ducking their beaks into the water and then tossing their heads upwards and standing back, preening themselves in self-admiration. You have to know your geese well to capture all of this in a painting, and this picture had it all.

I swallowed twice when I saw the price. Gabriel had no such reservations, but I was having a Scrooge day, so we came home without the picture. But I brought it home in my mind. The geese would not go away but stayed honking around in my head. I rang my friend Mary, who paints with me. She listened to my spiel and demanded to know, 'Have you the money?' When I confessed that I did, she said, 'Will you go back out the road and buy that bloody picture? Because if you don't, you will be forever bellyaching about it.'

The reason for her clear assessment of the situation was because a few years earlier there had been a similar situation, and my inner Scrooge had won. She had listened to me regretting it for months afterwards. So Mary knew what she was talking about. The following day, Gabriel and I went back out the road and bought the geese. I have never regretted it. Now I tuck the red berry holly in behind them. The geese and the small crib are a little bit of home.

The holly continues around the room, with red ribbons trailing along the branches. The tiny fragile crib made out of wood shavings finds its annual resting place on Aunty Peg's sideboard. Santa in a rickety sleigh lands on top of the grandfather clock. When all is done, I sit down in the glowing lights of the tree and watch the world go by.

The Royal Gift

When I opened the kitchen door, there it was, sitting on the table. A compact, firmly wrapped, small and square parcel. I approached it with curiosity and lifted it up to determine its contents. Not unduly heavy but yet I felt that it contained something of substance. I shook it. Not a rattle to be heard. It was as firmly self-contained as a leather *sliothar*. The little missive had the appearance that it could come hurling through space and still remain intact. There was no possibility that whatever was within could be damaged or even dented. This little parcel had been securely wrapped by a master wrapper.

But you cannot restrain a smell. It vaguely permeated the air around the little box. I sniffed. Then sniffed deeper. The odour evaded any specific identification by my senses. Then I took a deep inhalation that drew the smell down into my inner being. Very, very slowly, the faint aroma began to uncurl deep layers of memory. Somewhere in the remote pages of my mind, a thurible swung through the air. *Interesting*, I thought. The fascination with the parcel began to grow.

I am not a instant post-opener. If you are the receiver of envelopes with windows, I believe that those windows should remained firmly shut until after you have enjoyed early morning sustenance and should not be allowed to taint a good breakfast. If your post is of a more refreshing and uplifting nature, the process of disclosure should be savoured at a later time, not hurriedly submerged with porridge and marmalade. So, my little parcel remained on the kitchen table.

Breakfast over, I went about the enjoyable business of filling the bird feeders and having a meander around the garden to check up on what was going on out there. Every gardener knows that you go into the garden for a quick look around but you are still there a couple of hours later. Eventually, as the cold began to soak into my bones, I headed in for the warmth of the kitchen, where I assembled my lunch on a tray and carried it to the *seomra ciúin*.

I put my tray down on Mrs C's table. Mrs C spent fourteen of her twilight years with us before her final exit, and for me those years were a learning curve. 'Don't ever grow old, my dear,' she instructed in imperious tones with the air of one accustomed to being obeyed. 'It's a deplorable condition.' But she had mastered the art of growing old gracefully, and anything that made old age more bearable and comfortable she acquired. One of those acquisitions was a light, elegant coffee table on wheels. You may wonder about the wheels. But when muscles are stiff and movement is restricted, it is sometimes easier to move

an object than manipulate the body around it.

Mrs C's table has two levels. The lower shelf was for magazines, books and miscellaneous objects that needed to be within reaching distance. The top was a landing strip for trays carrying snacks and, in the evenings, Mrs C's cut-glass tumbler glinting with warm amber whiskey. The whiskey was one of her cushions against the ravages of old age but was never taken to excess, as that would have been against the rules of good behaviour in which she was a staunch believer. When she made her final exit, I inherited her whiskey table, and I soon realised what a well-thought-out acquisition it was. Restored and repolished, it slides like a ballerina at the slightest touch and is sometimes more mobile than its owner.

Before lunch, I had landed my precious parcel on Mrs C's table. She would have approved of the person who wrapped this parcel. She liked things done properly, and this parcel had been wrapped with the thoroughness of an expert. I tried to prise the firm adhesive tape from around the top with my fingers, but it defied my efforts. I had to withdraw to the kitchen and bring forth a vicious little kitchen devil. I slipped the blade in under the tape and cut neatly along the top. Two flaps rose simultaneously like wings released from bondage, and soft white tissue paper fluffed itself up. A deep and intriguing red colour glowed from within, and the rich aromatic smell of incense wafted out.

I delicately folded back the layers of tissue paper to reveal the most gorgeous deep-red candle. It smelt of benediction, convent chapels and cloistered monks. I eased out the beautiful candle from the depths of the little box, and the delicately waxed band around it informed me that the smell was frankincense. Frank-incense: the gift that the wise men had brought to Bethlehem from the East. What a gift! It was from a friend who creates the most amazing lightly scented handmade candles. Over the years, I had received lavender- and rose-scented candles from him, but this was the first frankincense one. On this week before Christmas, I felt blessed to have received such a wonderful gift. It was a link bridging the ages to Bethlehem. For the first Christmas ever I would not light the traditional white Irish candle but this rich, red, frankincense candle with roots stretching back to the origins of Christianity.

Elated by this wonderful gift I rang my friend straight away to tell him of my delight. I have learnt from experience that thanks should never be put on hold but let flow with the tide of gratitude. If put on hold, it could lose its spontaneity, or, worse still, never get done. Larry, whose little workshop and candle outlet is located in Bennettsbridge, Co. Kilk-enny, the home of much creativity, was delighted to hear about the reaction to his candle.

Years earlier, I had called to his workshop with a friend and never forgot the array of wonderful candles and essences that greeted us when we pushed open the door. It was magical. Since then, I make contact when my candle supply needs to be replenished. 'I had a lot of difficulty sourcing the requirements to make that frankincense candle,' he told me, 'and that one is just a trial sample. I sent it to you to see what you think.'

'Consider it an outstanding success,' I assured him.

'But you did not light it yet, did you?' he asked.

'Oh, not until Christmas night,' I told him, 'but judging by the smell, the feel and the gorgeous colour it cannot but be fantastic.'

'Well, so far so good anyway,' he laughed, 'but I will await the final judgement after lighting.'

'I'll report back,' I assured him, but I had absolute confidence in the success of his frankincense candle.

I normally put my traditional white Christmas candle in an old earthenware crock full of sand and surrounded it with red berry holly. This royal new-comer warranted a slightly different display. One of the pluses of being a collector (a more selective name for a hoarder) is that when a special occasion unex-pectedly occurs, you may have something that will rise to it. On my sideboard, which I inherited from

Aunty Peg, is a Waterford cut-crystal cake stand.

When my darling husband and I reached our fifteenth wedding anniversary, which is the crystal one, he decided to mark it with a crystal gift. He was standing outside Egan's in Cork, inspecting the window display for something suitable. Egan's was then one of the jewels of Patrick Street, with its mahogany and glass door and huge windows sparkling with Cork silver, cut glass and jewellery.

Who should appear beside him but my sister, who lives in another part of the country but who happened to be in Cork shopping that day. They put their heads together, and the result was this magnificent Waterford cut-glass cake stand, with which I was thrilled. Over the years, this cake stand became the bearer of christening cakes, Holy Communion cakes and birthday cakes. Now it was to be the bearer of a royal candle. I retrieved it from the sideboard, gave it a quick wash and polished it until it shone. It would do your heart good simply to look at it.

In recent times, beautiful cut crystal and fine bone china have gone out of fashion. But now they are making a comeback, as shown by the rise in popularity of tasteful tea rooms serving their customers afternoon tea in fine bone-china cups. Beautiful creations will always make a comeback.

I carried my cake stand to the hall and placed it

carefully on the old oak table where the Christmas candle normally stood. Bought years ago in a junk shop, for the princely sum of fourteen pounds, this table had been dirty and scruffy with a wobbly leg. It had cleaned up and restored well. Collectors never forget the price of a duck that turns out to become a swan; we tend to forget the ducks that continue to be lame ducks.

Then I brought my candle lovingly from Mrs C's table and placed it on the crystal where it reflected in its polished surface. I stood back to appraise the situation and decided that there was something missing. The table was not dancing with the crystal and candle. The whole thing was not in harmony. It needed more.

In the storeroom off my kitchen is Aunty Peg's linen press, which is packed with a huge variety of table linens and cloths of all variety and sizes. Aunty Peg loved collecting good table linen, and in me she had a willing accomplice. Over the years I have added to her collection, and now her press is bulging with all kinds of everything, which every few years takes a full day to sort out and tidy. When it is done I glow with a sense of achievement and satisfaction. It is a few years now since I enjoyed that glow. So it took a good root through the shelves to find what I was looking for.

Years ago, at a Christmas market in Prague, I bought a cloth. The rough feel of the unbleached linen and the cream fringing against a background of hand-embroidered red and gold holly wreaths was irresistible. It was fit for a royal table. My dull, solid little oak table disappeared beneath it and was transformed. On the cloth went the crystal and the crimson candle. These three belonged together.

Out in my back porch, together with my own holly, was red berry holly that a friend had brought me from the Black Valley. Something you get as a gift is somehow very special, and there is nothing to compare with the dark green glossy leaves of our native holly. When it decides to bear berries, they glow against the dark background. I gathered some of the red berries and laid them around the candle on the crystal stand, where they were reflected, connecting the candle with the wreaths on the cloth. My royal candle was suitably ensconced. It was ready and waiting for Christmas.

The Candle in
the Window

At the bottom of an old linen press in an upstairs corridor is a collection of earthenware crocks. They are cream-coloured and brown-rimmed, solid, heavy, and not easily overturned. They were acquired many years ago when a jam factory, Ogilvie & Moore of Cork, ceased production. At the time I was running a guest house and felt that my guests should enjoy the pleasure of home-made marmalade for their breakfasts. So, every January, into these four-pound crocks was poured a waterfall of golden marmalade.

That need is now gone, and my reduced marmalade-making can be contained in recycled honey jars. And so the earthenware crocks have found another function: they are now Christmas window candle containers. Filled with wet sand from the nearby strand in Garretstown, they make extremely secure candle-holders, safe enough to pass any health and safety test, I think. Not everybody is convinced of that, because each year one of my practical sons assures me that one Christmas I am going to burn down the entire menagerie. However, that has yet to happen so a few days before Christmas a visit to Garretstown beach is on the agenda.

The seaside in winter is a bracing experience, striding along the beach with the wind whipping around your ears, bringing your hair into a whirl and vibrating your ears with the sound of the water pounding off the rocks. When the cold begins to penetrate the bones, it is time to fill up the bucket with sand and head for home. I am probably in contravention of some EU regulation, but Christmas must override their rules as it was there long, long before them.

While collecting sand it is difficult to resist the urge to pick up interesting stones, shells and odd bits of wood that somehow will find a place in the decorating scheme. This pre-Christmas visit to the sea is a great stimulant as it washes out the cobwebs of the mind and prepares us to be blown indoors for Christmas.

On the day before Christmas Eve, it is time to visit the upstairs press, haul out the heavy crocks and bear them down the stairs to the kitchen table. We are told by fitness gurus that it is very good for your health and fitness to have a stairs in your house to provide regular exercise. That may well be, but this crock-carrying is a severe test of stickatitness.

By the time the crock-moving project is complete, the kitchen table is laden with array of crocked candles. First they get an overhaul: paring the candles to remove surplus wax and trimming the wicks to bring them onto a level lighting plane. Candles past their light-up time are replaced. In some of the jars, the sand has subsided, and this is topped up from the bucket of Garretstown sand. Then a tour of all the window sills, where the jars, with their firmly sand-secured candles, are put in place. They are totally safe from causing an inferno as the jars are heavy and full of sand so there is no danger of them falling over. The curtains are usually drawn well back as the light is meant to shine unhindered into the darkness when they are lit on Christmas night.

The window of the *seomra ciúin* is a special assignment. Normally it is the camping site for miscellaneous books and objects of no fixed abode, but now all is cleared for a new encampment: the wooden crib. The box containing the wooden crib is borne from the Christmas press back down the corridor, and as it is no lightweight it is a relief to land it on the floor beside the window. This is to be a street-facing crib rather than a room-facing one. And, because it faces out onto the street, it requires constant traipsing in and out of the nearby front door to ascertain progress.

The occupants of the original crib in Bethlehem had to simply move in, but this stable has to be created from scratch. And, because the landscape in Bethlehem was no rose garden and the stable no luxury hotel with fitted carpet, jute bags and rocks are used to depict a rugged terrain. The figures are not

the highly decorative models that grace more modern cribs but are solid, rugged, wooden interpretations of reality. There is no firm plan for the layout, but it begins with Mary and Joseph, then shepherds, a cow, a donkey and even camels brought from the Holy Land are gradually introduced. As the stable scene develops, it takes on a life of its own and is softened by winged angels and colourful birds. When all the personnel are in situ, two sand-filled jars with candles are placed in amongst them. Then lights are discreetly wound along between the rocks so that passing children can look in and enjoy the scene.

With all the windows holding a candle ready to be lit and to welcome Christmas, the final step is to hang the wreath on the front door. Over the years, the idea of a door wreath arose, was considered and was abandoned. Because we live on an extremely busy main road, the feasibility of the idea was questioned. Then, one year at DJ's open house, the perfect door wreath had proved too great a temptation. It was a swirl of fine feathery pine adorned with tory tops or pine cones, simply gorgeous. The first Christmas the wreath went up, a cynical neighbour gloomily predicted, 'That won't last long there.' But he was wrong, and every year the survival of this wreath maintains one's faith in the goodness of human nature. Christmas brings out the best in all of us.

The Sacred
Bridge

Back on the home farm, when I was a child, no decorations went up until Christmas Eve. It was the tradition of our house, and, I think, of all the neighbouring farmhouses at the time. That tradition is long gone, but I still feel that the month of the Holy Souls, as my mother termed November, belongs to them alone. Not a Christmas decoration is allowed to twinkle in my mind until the page showing December appears on the large calendar hanging on the back of my kitchen door. Before that, the only acknowledgement that Christmas is coming is the maturing mincemeat and puddings in Aunty Peg's press and the Advent wreath on the kitchen table on which I light a candle each morning before breakfast.

This wreath was a gift from my beloved sister Ellen, who lived most of her life in Toronto but who spent many Christmases with us until cancer stole her away, just before Christmas a few years ago. The wreath, as well as being an acknowledgement of Advent, is a remembrance of her. Maybe it is also the opening of the first page of the memory book that is so much part of Christmas.

Though November is the month of remembrance, Christmas brings the pain of loss to the surface, especially a recent loss. One year, the day before Christmas Eve, I heard a tentative knock on the door. Almost inaudible. I waited for a few seconds, wondering if I had imagined it. Then it came again, slightly more pronounced. I happened to be sitting at my laptop in the front room, with the door beside me open into the hallway. I went quickly and opened the front door. Nobody there. Usually when this happens, the person has gone around the corner to the side door, thinking that I may be in the kitchen out of hearing range of the front door.

And, sure enough, the knock came just as I went up the steps from the kitchen to the side door. I was surprised and delighted to find Audrey standing outside. As she lives at the other end of the parish, our paths do not cross that often. A beautiful young mother of two little boys, her husband had died of cancer during the year. It had been one of those deaths that had brought together the entire parish in a spontaneous flood of sympathy and support. Since then, despite her deep anguish, Audrey had carried about her a glow of inner peace and other-worldliness. This would be her first Christmas without her husband and her boys' first Christmas without their father. It was going to be a tough time for them.

She had come to get a book signed for her husband's uncle who enjoyed reading my books. We made our way to the *seomra ciúin* to find a pen on my desk. There we sat and talked while outside the window non-stop Christmas traffic poured past. Beside us the log fire crackled in the stillness of the room. Audrey talked, and I listened. I knew better than to be a Johnny-Fix-It. Johnny-Fix-Its are no help to the bereaved.

Every road through grief winds its own painful journey. Audrey's pain was tangible. Married to the love of her life for fifteen years, though they were sometimes overshadowed by his illness, they had shared wonderful love and togetherness. During that illness, Audrey, with her medical knowledge and warm personality, had been a tower of strength, carrying her two boys through the trauma of parting with their beloved father. Now that he was gone, she was stretching out to cover both parental roles. She was blessed to have two wonderfully supportive families, her husband's and her own, and to be surrounded by a great community. It all helps, but when you grieve, your grief is your own. She carried it in the deep core of her being.

That evening, my friend Maura called, bearing a box. 'Don't be misled by the box,' she cautioned. 'It is only a few home-mades.' But, to me, home-made is as good as it gets. Maura too had buried her husband during the year, and, while still deep in that grief, she had suffered the loss of another family member.

She was endeavouring to be strong to support her bereaved daughter.

Maura is one of those dependable people who every year on Hospice Coffee Morning comes laden with her wonderful home baking. She is as constant as the Northern Star. Now, even though struggling to cope with the grind of constant sorrow, she had taken the time to make some of her wonderful baking in appreciation of the little bits of comfort we had exchanged over the past few months. Generous people like Maura are the living spirit of Christmas.

Later, I sat by the fire and thought of how difficult the prospect of Christmas can be for people who have been thrust onto the harsh road of grief during the year. Christmas looms up ahead like a towering roadblock that has to be scaled. The first time I had been in that position was a gut-wrenching experience. We were not in the aftermath of death that time but were waiting in its approaching shadow. A few days before that Christmas, our much-loved cousin Con, who had spent many Christmases with us, was diagnosed with terminal cancer. He was a quiet, gentle man. Many years earlier, when he began teaching in a school in a nearby town, he came to stay for a while. The 'while' turned into years, during which time he became part of our family. He was an oasis of peace and tranquillity in the midst of our busy household and was a listening

ear and comforter in times of stress.

That year, he taught in his school up to the Christmas holidays, and then the bombshell came. Having gone to the doctor with what he thought was a bad flu, the diagnosis fell like the blow of a sledgehammer. His two brothers, who were priests in Dublin and Belfast, came to stay, and that night, as we gathered to light the Christmas candle, we all knew that it would be the last time for one of the circle around our hall table. Later that night, his brothers concelebrated mass in our church. I can still remember the deep pain and the sacredness of that mass.

A few years later, my husband Gabriel died suddenly in late November. After the initial shock, we gradually began to gather our wits about us. But Christmas loomed like a menacing spectre on the horizon. How would we cope with our grief in the midst of all the remembering and celebrations of previous Christmases? The dreaded hurdle proved surprisingly manageable, and, when the time came, mixed with the acute pain came unexplainable rays of divine ease. The prospect had been worse than the reality.

Another time, a few years after that again, I was in Heathrow on Christmas Eve, on my way to Toronto to spend Christmas with my sister. Due to an unexpected diagnosis, she was unable to travel. For years she had come home to Innishannon for Christmas, and now my daughter and I were travelling to bring home over to her. That Christmas morning in Toronto, we walked to mass through snow-covered streets, and the following night we went to the ballet and watched a magical performance of *The Nutcracker*. I can honestly say it is one of my loveliest memories. Mixed with the deep pain of impending departure was the sharing of this beautiful ballet.

The following year, after months of unsuccessful chemotherapy, I again travelled to Toronto to spend Christmas with her. It was not to be. She died in mid-December, and we brought her ashes home to Innishannon before Christmas. In grief, our senses are tuned in to the delicate fabric of another zone. At Christmas, Heaven moves a little closer, and a sacred bridge spans both worlds. On that holy night, our departed loved ones come closer.

Christmas Eve

When we were young, by the time Christmas Eve came we were like a tide held back by a strong wall that was now to burst open with a huge surge of enthusiasm. There was no holding us back. The house decorating, which had been held off until then, was about to begin. Bundles of holly and ivy were swept into the kitchen, and we buried everything in greenery.

My mother, ignoring all the mayhem around her, calmly began the ritual of stuffing the goose. Before the stuffing could commence, the goose was singed over a lighted paper – white for a cleaner flame – on the flagstone in front of the fire to remove any traces of soft downy wisps still clinging to its skin. Singeing had to be done swiftly and with perfect timing. The aim was to have a clear flame beneath the goose and to proceed with fast jerky movements. This was no time for slow motion because if you were not a fast mover you could finish up with a multicoloured goose. With the arrival of methylated spirits this became an easier task as the blue flame was clean and easy to manage. The exercise filled the kitchen with the whiff of scorched feathers. Afterwards, any tiny infringements that had escaped the inferno were diligently removed.

Earlier that day my mother had boiled a black pot
of potatoes over the open fire, and when the potatoes began to break through their jackets, she swung
the pot off the hangers and strained away the boiling water. When the potatoes were sufficiently cool
to be peeled in comfort, a large green enamel dish
was filled with steaming white floury potato while
a galvanised bucket beside it filled up with skins. On
top of the mound of potato she landed a generous
lump of yellow butter which slowly melted, streaming
down between the potatoes. Then came a waterfall
of cooked onions, the peeling of which had brought
a waterfall of tears down her face. All these were
churned into a soft stuffing mixture. If she judged the
mixture to be too dry she carefully added a few drops
of liquid from the saucepan of cooked giblets boiled
the night before and left to cool.

In another enamel basin my mother had put
breadcrumbs made from the insides of a stale two-
pound loaf to which she now added salt, pepper, cinnamon, mixed herbs and a very limited amount of
sage. (She judged sage to be hard on the digestive
system.) These herbs she rubbed between her palms
just as my father rubbed the layers of tobacco he
peeled off his plug prior to filling his pipe. Into this
mixture she grated a large green cooking apple saved
from my grandmother's apple trees, which annually

produced a large crop. She might then add a pinch of caster sugar to balance the flavour. If it was still not to her satisfaction, another dribble of the giblet juice could be added.

When the entire mixture was judged to be sufficiently flavoursome and of the correct consistency, she took it to the lower room off the kitchen, which, with its sub-zero temperature, was the nearest thing we had to a fridge. When the stuffing had completely cooled in the freezing temperatures of this room, my mother began the ritual of stuffing the goose. First to be done was the breast cavity and then the body. To prevent either bursting while cooking, she allowed sufficient room for expansion. Then, like a master surgeon, she stitched up her patient with her largest darning needle threaded with a soft white flax cord.

This cord had been the stitching along the tops of the flour bags when they came from the mill. It was carefully eased out when opening the bags, wound up into little balls and stored away in my mother's sewing box for special jobs such as stitching up the Christmas goose. Because it was soft, it did not cut into the flesh of the goose, and it was less inclined to rip open in the cooking. My mother considered it better than her No. 10 sewing thread, which, though stronger than a No. 40, was a bit too rigid and unforgiving for the soft skin of her goose.

First to be stitched up was the breast, where my mother had allowed an ample flap for covering over the opening. The finished effect was neat, firm and almost invisible. Her sealing of the larger rear cavity was an exercise in master surgery in which she took huge pride. When the operation on her goose was complete, she stood back with a look of immense satisfaction on her face. The patient was then removed from the operating table, placed into the large green dish and covered with a well-washed, sun-bleached flour bag. The surplus stuffing was put into an earthenware basin and covered with butter paper held in place by a length of flax cord. The goose and the bowl were then laid to rest on a table in the lower room to await the big day.

Already sitting on the table in the lower room was the ham. The previous morning it had been retrieved from the top of the barrel of pickle and well washed to remove all traces of salt. A salty ham was not to my mother's liking. Then it was put into one of her heavy black pots and boiled gently for a long period over the fire. There was no set time for this boiling period; long years of experience guided the time, and when my mother judged that it was sufficiently cooked she swung the pot off the fire and carried it carefully to the chilly regions of the lower room, where she left it standing in its own water. There it rested overnight.

In the morning, she lifted it out of the pot and laid it on a large dish. She carefully eased off the skin and, with a large knife, criss-crossed the surface, creating diamonds. She then proceeded to plant a clove in each diamond. She mixed breadcrumbs, brown sugar and mustard, and, if the mixture was too dry, she added a few drops of the giblet water to bring it to the right consistency. She laid a coat of the mixture over the top of the ham, which was then returned to the empty pot and given a quick roast over the fire. Now the ham and goose lay in repose on the table in the lower room, on either side of the extra bowl of stuffing, all ready for the big occasion.

While my mother was thus engaged, we poked branches of holly behind holy pictures, between the bannisters of the stairs and along the meat hooks in the ceiling. Paper chains were strung around the kitchen, and a pleated paper went around the turnip holding the Christmas candle. It was my father's job to procure the biggest turnip in the pit and scoop a hole in it to hold the large candle.

When my mother judged that some of our exuberance was satisfied and that it was safe to introduce them, she went up to the parlour press and brought down what she called her Christmas mottos. These were old cardboard Christmas scenes which had been in the house for many years. They had survived

because she kept them safely locked up. One of them was a jovial Santa handing out parcels to rosy-faced children dressed in fancy fur capes. They definitely were not Irish children, so these pictures had probably been sent home from America by an emigrant relation.

From the wooded fairy fort behind our house came a huge block of wood off a fallen tree: the *blockeen na Nollag* my grandmother called it. This lay across the back of the open fire and would keep it glowing for the twelve days of Christmas. Resting against it were sods of black turf with red flames licking out between them. As dusk gathered in, the radio was turned on, and we listened carefully to hear Santa call out the names of all the children he was about to visit. We breathed a sigh of relief when we all featured on his list. Most children at the time were called after their ancestors, so Santa was on pretty safe ground with traditional names.

Then we went out and stood on the doorstep to look across the valley at the distant Kerry mountains and imagine we could see Santa with his sleigh and reindeers gliding along the peaks as he made his rounds. We also saw my father, bearing a bundle of hay on his back to the sheep in the field down by the river. The sheep were the only animals to be out overnight, just as it was on the first Christmas. Out in the stalls the cows were contentedly chewing the cud and the horses crunching hay from their mangers. An occasional cluck could be heard from the hens on their perches. Mother goose and the gander were home alone; their work for the year in providing many Christmas dinners was done.

With all the farm animals locked up for the night, it was time for the Christmas Eve supper. The normal fare of brown bread was ditched, and we savoured the luxury of sweet cake, butter loaf and seed loaf. Some of these had been gifted to us by shopkeepers in town and were deeply appreciated. Toast was part of our Christmas supper tradition, and the bread was toasted in front of the now red glowing sods of turf. Plates of golden toast streaming with yellow butter joined the barmbrack and cake making a rare appearance on our table.

Before any of the niceties that had our mouths watering could be tasted, the Christmas candle had to be lit. To my mother, the lighting of the candle was the official opening of the door into Christmas. An aura of peace and joy at the sacredness of the season surrounded her at this time. The candle was secure on the sill of the kitchen window. It stood tall, slim, white and elegant, embedded in a large yellow turnip edged around with a red paper skirt that sprouted twigs of dark green glossy holly glistening with red berries.

My father lit the candle, and my mother sprinkled

us with holy water. The candle cast a pool of light over the little cardboard crib on the sill beside it. One year, this crib had suddenly appeared in the window of our local shop. It had brought us to a standstill. We stood with our noses pressed against the glass, peering in at it in awe. Finally we plucked up the courage to go in and enquire as to the price. Two shillings? A huge sum in our eyes. How were we to procure it? But there is no barrier that can hold back a dream. And we had a dream: a dream that this crib should be part of our Christmas.

We went home and thought about it. Maybe if we pooled all our resources? We each had a money box to hold any donations that came our way, such as 'stands' from visiting relatives or rare pennies earned for doing jobs for neighbours. Between all these little contributions, we might have enough. We emptied all our money boxes, and between us we came up with the two shillings. Now we swelled with pride as we viewed our investment in its place beside the Christmas candle.

When supper was over, it was time to play the new records that were part of every Christmas. My father got them in the local shop, and no matter what he bought we thought they were great. The gramophone was normally resident on the parlour sideboard, but for Christmas it was a welcome visitor to the kitchen. We played the new records non-stop, but when their novelty had worn a bit thin, we went back to the old favourites. John McCormack, Fr Sydney Mac-Ewan, Josef Locke, Delia Murphy and many others warbled around our kitchen. We savoured every note and eventually learnt the words of their songs. Then it was time for lemonade and biscuits. The red lemonade came in small glass bottles, and with it we crunched the rare treat of Kerry Cream biscuits. To our delight, the lemonade fizzed down our noses and caused our eyes to water.

Meanwhile, my mother made the trifle for the next day's dinner. She took a large red bowl from the parlour press and placed it on the kitchen table. It was a seldom used cut-glass bowl she had inherited from her mother. We knew it was one of her treasures. Into this she placed circles of sponge cake, layered with strawberry jam and tinned pears to which my father was partial. The contents were then generously laced with sherry. Red jelly, already melted in a ware jug and allowed to cool slightly, was poured over the contents of the bowl, which soaked it all up. Tomorrow it would be covered with custard or cream skimmed off the top of the churn. The thought of it made our insides glow.

We did not want to go to bed and end this lovely night, but the thought that Santa might pass by if we were still up persuaded us. After a reluctant recitation of the rosary, we hung our stockings off the black crane by the fire and off the backs of the *sugán* chairs. Getting to sleep was not easy, and we fought against it, hoping to catch sight of Santa. There was a fireplace in our bedroom, and we hoped that we might catch sight of a red leg as Santa made his way down the chimney to the kitchen. But exhaustion won the day, and we were fast asleep when he finally passed down.

Some say that Christmas is really only for children as if with the sophistication of adulthood we should leave such simplistic belief behind us. And yet, dormant within each one of us are the roots of the child we once were. At Christmas that child reawakens and we again believe that the impossible is possible. So, after much preparation, Christmas Eve finally arrives and opens wide the door into Christmas. All the getting ready is over, and there is no more donkey work to be tackled.

The day before Christmas Eve is when I stuff the turkey. I use a breadcrumb stuffing, to which I add a generous supply of grated apple and carrot and a generous amount of thyme and mixed herbs, and I cover my turkey with butter and streaky rashers. Then it is consigned to the chilly regions of the back porch. After that, the cranberry sauce is whipped together. I love home-made cranberry sauce, and it is so simple to make, simply throwing a packet of fresh cranberries, the juice of an orange and some caster sugar into the liquidiser. When that is done, the vegetables are prepared, and that's the mundane jobs out of the way.

The ham is brought to the boil in a pot of water on top of the Aga, then consigned to the bottom oven for a couple of hours. It is then removed and left to rest overnight in its mustardy clove water. As soon as I hit the kitchen on Christmas Eve morning, I lift it into a roasting tin, remove its leathery jacket, lather it with mustard, honey and breadcrumbs and baptise it with cider. Then I hand it over into the loving care of the Aga, the grande dame of the kitchen. I love the smell that oozes around the kitchen as she slowly cooks it.

Having lit the fire in the *seomra ciúin* and switched on the lights of the tree and the cribs around the house, I enjoy a leisurely breakfast and open the last of the Christmas cards. If any are especially nice, I give them pride of place on the line of cards hanging across the kitchen. I bring out my Christmas Eve tablecloth, bought in a Salzburg Christmas market. When I spread its gorgeous red candles embroidered on bleached linen over the table, it breathes Christmas. It is time now for doing nothing but enjoying callers and chatting.

In the afternoon, I stroll up the hill to visit the family grave. In the churchyard, many of the graves are glowing with glossy holly wreaths and fresh flowers. It is obvious from the thoughtful arrangements that

people are remembering. Standing by our grave, I too remember and ask for guidance from those wonderful people who were once part of my life. My grandmother believed that the gates of Heaven are open on Christmas night, and who am I to contradict her? In any case, she was a woman not open to being contradicted. Looking at the names of the people I have loved on the headstone creates a link between our worlds, and there is a sense that the gap between them has indeed narrowed. I come down the hill feeling at peace with both of these worlds.

Then it is candle-lighting time. The ideal is that some of the family gather for the lighting of the main candle, which is in the hallway, and that we carry that light around to the candles in all the windows of the house. However, over the years this has proved unachievable as gathering some of my unwieldy gaggle together before dusk is a mammoth undertaking. Needless to mention, there are endless last-minute jobs to be done. So we leave the lighting of the real Christmas candle until later.

Now, as dusk descends, I go around the house at my leisure and light the candles in all the windows. I love lighting the candles in the windows. Ours is a corner house in the centre of a village on the main road to West Cork, and it is nice to have the candles glowing for passers-by as they go home for Christmas. Around the house, other candles are lit – there is something very restful and peaceful about candlelight. This all leads to one son's seasonal observation that one year we will all go up in smoke, but I am very careful with them and so far so good. It's been going on for a long time.

When we gather to light the main candle, we have the tradition of singing 'Silent Night', a practice started by an English lady who spent many Christmases with us. She was a wonderful singer. With her departure, the calibre of the performance declined, but though we may not be of high choral standard, we still do it. It is a time for remembering because we have done this in the same place for years, and over that time many who were there for the different Christmas candle-lightings are no longer with us. For these moments, as the candle flickers into a glow, they come close to us, and as I sprinkle holy water, a practice inherited from my mother, the past and the present join hands. It is a sacred moment.

Then it is supper time, and the ham is opened for tasting, and I discover if I did a good job. Here in Innishannon, we have an early mass, which is called the children's mass, and the church overflows with families and children of all ages. The little ones make their presence felt – in other words, there is pure bedlam. Although I contributed hugely to that bedlam in my time, I am now into peace and quiet enjoyment, so I go up the hill to the late mass, which we call the midnight mass although it takes place a bit before that time.

This to me is the heart of Christmas. I simply love this mass. The church has a special atmosphere, a sense of the sacred. The choir, as if inspired by the occasion, reaches new heights, and on that night the Christmas hymns that have been belted out in piped music for months around every commercial corner finally come into their own. This is where these hymns truly belong. In the quietened hush after Holy Communion, our soloist, Sinead, who has the voice of an angel, gives a rendition of 'Holy Night' that always makes me feel that this is the bridge to the gate my grandmother believed was open on Christmas night.

It is lovely then to walk down the hill onto the quiet village street. Normally the traffic through our village is non-stop, but on Christmas night we have the place to ourselves. Well, almost. There is always someone going somewhere. Afterwards, we gather around the kitchen table with some friends and neighbours for a late supper and chat. When they all are gone home, I like to sit in the candlelit stillness of the house and just absorb the peace of the night. It's Christmas.

Christmas Day

On Christmas morning at the home farm, we awoke with a thump of excitement. It was still dark, but we jumped out of bed and tumbled down the high narrow stairs. The only light in the kitchen was the glow of the Sacred Heart lamp and the fading embers of the fire, but we were directed by anticipation and instinct. Bulging stockings yielded up oranges, apples, crayons and colouring books. Games of ludo and snakes and ladders brought forth squeals of delight, and one year I got a new school satchel into which I eagerly buried my face for the fresh leather smell. Sometimes a soft cloth doll or wooden toys were danced around the kitchen, and Meccano was yanked out of boxes. No matter what we got, there was wild excitement.

When we calmed down, a discussion was held as to who would walk the three miles into early mass in order to be home to mind the goose that my mother would by then have put in the bastible over the fire. I always volunteered because I loved the walk in the silent world of frost and stillness, and when we reached the top of the hill we stood at the gate onto the road and counted the Christmas candles flickering in the windows along the valley. Normally the valley would be clothed in darkness, but this was Christmas. Christmas was different. And Christmas was magic.

After the dark road, the church was glowing with light. We were bursting with excitement to see the crib – after all, this was what it was all about. First there was mass to get through. We thought that it would never end. When the priest left the altar, we made a beeline for the crib but had to take our place in the long queue, craning our necks around bulky adults to get a peep. Finally, we were there, standing in front of the Baby Jesus, Mary, Joseph, the shepherds, the cow and the donkey, all nestled down into golden straw with the star sparkling down on them. We loved it and dropped our big brown pennies into the box to help Jesus do whatever it was he needed to do.

On arrival home, it was then our job to change the coals on the cover of the bastible with the long iron tongs and watch all the pots my mother had left cooking around the fire. Earlier, she had swung the bastible over the built-up fire, and when it was heated she laid her goose into it. It was important to get it off to a good hot start, otherwise we could finish up with a pale, uncooked goose. Then she covered it with the 'veil' saved from the killing of the pig. The veil was part of the lining of the pig's stomach, which looked like a net curtain of circles of fat held together by a transparent veil. If she did not have a veil from her own pigs, she procured one from Danny the Butcher in town. During cooking, the veil kept the goose moist and tender. (We had no knowledge of cholesterol to worry us.) The heated lid went on top of the bastible, and around this she laid a circle of hot coals. When she had gone to mass, it was our job to regularly change the hot coals on the cover and to keep the fire well banked up with turf and logs beneath it.

First, it was time for breakfast, and on the table was the large ham with its glazed mustard and bread-crumb coat. My brother carefully carved slices, and we savoured it with delight, knowing that there was more to come later. We tidied up the kitchen that was now filling with the aroma of roast stuffed goose and entertained ourselves by playing all the new records and exploring our new toys. When my mother arrived home, there was a flurry of getting everything ready for the Christmas dinner. We were usually sitting by the time the King's Speech began, at 3pm. Every year, the King, and later his daughter, the present queen, was part of our Christmas dinner. In later years, turkey became fashionable in Ireland, but to me nothing ever again tasted as good as that Christmas goose, floating in a sea of golden grease and oozing rolls of gorgeous potato stuffing. It was probably a dietician's nightmare, but oh boy did it taste good.

After dinner, Santa's generosity was spread all over

the kitchen floor. We played ludo and snakes and ladders and fought over the rules of the game, with my mother acting as peace negotiator. Colouring books were filled in and fairy stories were read. Later, my father – probably glad of the break – slipped out to see to the cattle, and when he came back in it was time for supper. Despite the gigantic dinner, we were quite ready for it.

Afterwards, we played cards, and this could sometimes lead to World War III. Eventually my mother called it a day and got us all on our knees for the rosary. With the calming repetition of the rosary came peace, quiet and the realisation that a tidal wave of tiredness was about to submerge us. We all trailed up the dark steep stairs bearing sconces with candles. It was always a day to remember. The memories of our childhood Christmases sleep within us for the rest of our lives, and every Christmas awaken with a blend of mystery and magic. Then the Christmas Past and Christmas Present, the believable and the unbelievable dance together. Heaven and Earth join hands, and our celebrations are the bridge linking those two worlds.

A slow awakening is surely a highly desirable entrance into any new day. The mind and body were never meant to crash suddenly into the morning but rather to rise slowly like the cow out in the field. The wise cow slowly chews the cud and ruminates for a long time before rising in slow stretching stages into an upright position. Having limbered her muscles into a long easy stretch, she swishes her tail to get that end loosened up, then shakes her head into a neck massage and slowly ambles in unperturbable harmony with her body across the field. She is now ready for the day ahead.

On Christmas morning, I imitate the cow. Having come to full consciousness, I wonder will I chance turning on the radio. On weekdays, I never turn on the radio before getting out of bed as I have no desire to face world problems while still in a vulnerable, prone position. Weekends are different as, for some reason, the airwaves are less intent on crucifying us with national and global problems before we are ready to face our own little corner of the world.

I decide against meeting the outside world before finding out the state of my own mind and body. I need to meet myself first before having the world thrust upon me. The early morning is about investigating the state of your mind and body, and if they are not up to par taking the time necessary to bring them into sync with each other. After a little time ruminating, I ease myself into a sliding position and find myself upright on the floor. The aim of this exercise is to get myself downstairs to put the turkey into the oven. Once that is done, I will decide on the next step.

In the kitchen, the Aga opens her arms in warm welcome. Here she is the matriarch, and she runs her domain with a warm but firm hand. A multitasker, she is undoubtedly female. She can boil, simmer, steam, oven roast and keep warm every pot or pan put upon her or into her, all at the same time. Though strong and powerful, she has the delicate temperament of a finely bred racehorse. If she is out of kilter the whole house is out of kilter. She heats all the water, and when she is in good form it steams out of every tap. She will snort and belch in protest if, after her once-a-year service, she is not perfectly retuned, and leave us out in the cold. But she and my Aga man have a perfect understanding and dance together in complete harmony. Over the years, she and I have become firm friends and have honed a great working relationship. She is the boss, and I humour her every whim.

At Christmas, she comes into her own. This morning she is glowing with cooperation and receives the turkey into the warm embrace of her top department and the plum pudding and bowl of stuffing into her lower one, telling me to go away now about my business as this is her job.

Following her orders, I put my breakfast on a tray and take it upstairs to my bedroom. I love breakfast in bed. A rare treat, it breathes relaxation and dawdling. Dawdling is good for the soul. As I partake of grapefruit and porridge, I chance putting on the radio and am delighted to find Christmas readings and music. Not a bomb or a bullet to be heard. Hopefully they are all taking a leaf out of the book of the soldiers in the First World War who ceased firing on each other and walked across no man's land to wish each other a happy Christmas. It was a ray of light in a very dark place, kindling a faint hope of forgiveness and peace. Even though in their hearts they knew it could not be, the soldiers still felt the need for some light and hope.

Breakfast complete, I pick up my journal and spend some time meandering on to the page. Early morning is a most imaginative and creative time as the mind is as yet unpolluted with practicalities. William Blake, some time between 1757 and 1827, told us that imagination is evidence of the divine. Who are we to contradict him? But often our minds are too overloaded to receive divine or imaginative intervention.

A dip into a tattered book of poems, well thumbed by use, that I got from a sister who enjoys second-hand bookshops, and a browse through some well-loved favourites. Then a chapter from Deepak Chopra's *Seven Spiritual Laws of Success*. He is a spiritual teacher and writer who rings many meaningful bells for me.

With no more reasons left for procrastination, I get out of bed and, for some unknown reason, open the small drawer of a dressing table. There, stored carefully

away in tissue paper, is the little cardboard crib that we sisters bought between us many years ago. I am absolutely delighted to come upon it. It is like meeting an old friend.

I eventually make it downstairs, where I do a bit of a tidy-up, light the fire and place the little crib on the hall table. Then for a stroll around the garden to see how things are out there and to wish them all a happy Christmas. The holly trees look smart and spruced up after their seasonal trim. This is their time at centre stage, with no showy flowering neighbours to steal their limelight.

Back inside, the fire is getting a grip, inviting me to sit down with feet up and have a look into the book I bought myself for Christmas. An hour later, it is time to think of putting on the dinner, which is usually targeted for around three. If it is ready well before that time or runs well after it, a gap could arise to listen to the Queen's Speech. Listening to the Queen's Speech was a tradition to which my father adhered, and for me it is part of Christmas. It does not always work out as the synchronising of the Queen and myself is totally a matter of chance. Unlike me, she holds steadfast to her 3pm deadline.

A quick peep in at the turkey, which is on the point of losing its legs. This tells me that it is removal time. It emerges brown and beautiful, and my matriarch Aga

smirks in I-told-you-so satisfaction. On her and into her go all the various pots and pans, and, as they come to the boil, simmer and roast, I begin to lay the table for dinner. I am a tablecloth person, so I open Aunty Peg's linen press and out comes one of her best cloths, accompanied by a set of table napkins embroidered with the reindeer names bought in Toronto with my sister. Off the dresser comes the dinner service inherited from Aunty Peg with all the necessary tureens and side plates to make a table statement.

An old nun in Drishane Convent told us many years ago that before people put a bite into their mouths they eat with their eyes. Presentation is everything. I agree with her. As I enjoy the table dressing, I am joined by four-year-old Ellie, who insists on helping by putting forks out backwards and announcing that she should get the table napkin with the nicest reindeer. From there on, peace and quiet evaporate, and law and order break down. It is delegation time for cream-whipping, bottle-opening and cracker-arranging. Eventually all are seated, and, before formation collapses, grace before meals is said in English and, if we have a *Gaeilgeoir* amongst us, in Irish too.

Every year, the Christmas menu is totally predictable, almost a replica of the one my mother cooked, with the only major change being that the goose is replaced by a turkey. Otherwise, all remains the same, as in countless homes around the country. Where Christmas is concerned, we are mostly creatures of habit. The one surprise on this table could be the plum pudding, which varies from year to year because the making of it involves throwing everything into it that remains after cake and mincemeat making. A strong dose of rum in the making and a crown of flaming brandy on arrival at the table mask any shortcomings.

After dinner, it is present-opening time, which evolves into sheer bedlam. I fancy myself as a Gaelic coffee-maker supreme, which is probably totally unfounded and is due solely to the fact that it was I who first introduced it to our house after seeing the recipe on a tea towel in a little shop window down the street, which is now long gone. In more recent years, a more expert son-in-law has taken over the ritual. With the distribution of the Gaelic coffees there is a general collapse into varying stages of inertia.

When the family were teenagers, this was card-playing time, with a game of a hundred and ten being fought out to the bitter end. Those days are gone, and now it is the more civilised Scrabble and various other forms of distraction that peter out into exhausted termination. Finally the unanimous conclusions come that the beds are calling, and after a bedraggled supper there is a general scattering. Then I am home alone to sip a Gaelic coffee and read a book by the fire.

Between the Christmases

In old Ireland, between the Christmases the countryside slept. The land ceased production, giving man and animal time to rest. Land workers went home on Christmas Eve and did not return until the first day of February. Their work was done, and it was time to recuperate after the hard physical demands of the year. Winter ploughing was carried out in November and spring ploughing was yet to begin.

The days between the Christmases were a total contrast to the rest of the year as there was no early rising, which was the norm for farm living. The cows, who dictated the pace of farm life, were going through the lethargy of awaiting motherhood. Instead of demanding early milking, which was the financial lifeblood of the land, they were now satisfied to lie contentedly in their warm stalls where later in the day they would be fed and watered. This afforded people the opportunity to have a sleep-in, which led to late nights. Card-playing and music-making went on into the early hours of the morning.

While the land rested, people rested. Foreign holidays were not on the agenda, so people simply stayed put, slept late and visited each other. On St Stephen's

Day, in age-old Irish tradition, the young went out hunting the wren, travelling around the countryside in outrageous costumes and entertaining people with singing and dancing. They announced their arrival at the door with a song:

The wran, the wran, the king of all birds,
St Stephen's Day was caught in the furze
Up with the kettle and down with the pan
Give us the money to bury the wran.

The householders gave them money, supposedly for burying the wren, but which was spent providing drinks and eats for house dances where local musicians got an opportunity to display their talents.

In North Cork along the Kerry border, the land was not good and emigration was part of the way of life. With small farms and large families it was an accepted necessity. Those who had gone to England were regular visitors, but many of the local young lads went to America, mainly to Oregon. That was a long voyage then, taking over six weeks. When they arrived there, they were sent out onto the prairies to herd sheep and cattle. This was a tough lonely life for young fellows who had left large families and neighbourhoods rich with people. They ended up camping out alone on the prairies where they existed for months without human companionship. The money was good, but the cost in human isolation was high. Some settled down in Oregon, buying their own ranches with the money they made, while others returned home and bought farms.

Some of these emigrants occasionally made it home for Christmas, which was a cause for celebration amongst the families and, indeed, for the neighbours too. For the returning men it was a chance to relieve the months of isolation out in the prairies and to combat the loneliness for home that many must have felt. The locals held the Oregon Man's Dance to welcome them back. It was a great occasion for the locals too, a chance to meet up and celebrate the end of year. The timing was perfect as everybody was free to enjoy the occasion. For the rural women, it was a chance to dress up and have a good time dancing the night away.

There was a whiff of romance off these young men, with their large Stetson hats, locally known as Oregon man's hats. Sometimes romances blossomed, and the men went back to Oregon with new brides. For those of us who were very young it was all wildly romantic, with a touch of *Seven Brides for Seven Brothers*. Later, when we were teenagers, it was the dance on St Stephen's Night that lit up our lives between the Christmases. Some of our contemporaries were home on holiday from foreign parts and also from board-ing school and college, and this made life much more interesting. Romances blossomed then too, but there was no heading overseas afterwards.

On New Year's Eve, my mother lit another tall white candle in the kitchen window to welcome in the New Year, and the following day we had our second roast goose dinner. Then, on the eve of Little Christmas, the third candle was lit. This night had a special sense of mystery as it was believed that this was the night when water was turned into wine at the Wedding Feast of Cana. We viewed the white enamel bucket full of spring water with caution in case some-thing mysterious had taken place within. However, the following morning it was still plain water from the Fairy Well by the fort.

On Little Christmas Day, we concluded the season with another roast goose dinner. Little Christmas is also called Nollaig na mBan, Women's Christmas, and I remember Gabriel buying gifts for me and my sister Ellen on this day. The following day, we took down the decorations. It was a no-no to do so any sooner – you waited for the season to reach its conclusion. That week, the school reopened.

For me, the days between the Christmases are still a time to enjoy doing nothing. Our bodies are suffering from an avalanche of enrichments from which they need time to recover, and our stomach boundaries have been stretched far beyond their normal limits. It is the time for a little realignment. After the Christmas dinner there is a surplus of food, and this eliminates the need for cooking. Leftovers are a blessing. We use up a lot of time catering for the needs of our stomach, and with that requirement eliminated, a whole lot of free time floats into our lives. Time to do nothing. The mornings, instead of being a starting point to the working day, can be a slow awakening into a world of dawdling. Time to discover the magic of the morning, and days to be idled away doing whatever pleases you.

Let me unfold gently
Into a new day
As the sun calmly
Edging above the horizon
Before blazing into a dazzling dawn;
As the birds softly
Welcome the light
Before bursting into
The full dawn chorus;
As the cow rising
And stretching into
Her own body
Before bellowing
To her companions.

May I, too, slowly absorb,
Be calmed and centred
By the unfolding depths
Of this new day,
So that my inner being
Will dance in harmony
With whatever
It may bring.

It is all over. The time has arrived to take down Christmas. Back on the home farm, that was a simple enough procedure as the decorations consisted mainly of holly and ivy, which we simply whipped down and threw into the large open fire, where they burst into leaping flames, enveloped in a swirl of red and blue. No worry about a chimney fire as it was clean as a whistle after Black Ned's visit.

The tree branch was returned to the grove from whence it had come and left to shed its pines. Later, it was used to block a gap or make a perch in the hen house. The most elaborate of the cards were stored away for next year's Christmas tree, just in case next year's American cards did not prove as exciting as this year's. The gramophone was returned to the sideboard in the parlour, and my mother's mottos carefully stored away in the parlour press. We children were reluctant to see Christmas go. The balloons were burst. The show was over.

In this house, taking down the Christmas is a bit more long-tailed as my Christmas has accumulated a lot of attachments. Amongst them is the crib that I bought with my first pay packet, and also the little cardboard one that predates it and which is now so crippled by old age that it can scarcely stand. From those humble beginnings my Christmas has grown in stature over the years. Now, however, her bags have to be packed, and she has to go. It is like parting with an old friend. But the time has come for this friend to depart. There is nothing more tired-looking than droopy Christmas decorations, and by the seventh of January they are all beginning to lose their glow. Mrs C used to say that visitors who outstayed their welcome were like fish who were around for too long. Christmas fits into that category. It is time to say goodbye.

Christmas is a royal guest, who does not stoop to lowly tasks. She leaves to her host the mundane exercise of undressing and tucking her finery away into boxes. The empty boxes are retrieved from the Christmas press and laid out at specific points, and the marathon task of taking down Christmas begins. The putting-up begins with the crib, but the taking-down starts with the tree, which is by now looking a trifle overburdened with her elaborate finery.

First to be removed is her headdress, comprising of

the fairy queen in her flowing red dress and glittering crown. She is laid to rest in her long narrow coffin-like box. This is not a final parting as next Christmas she will rise again. Then down along the tiered branches, her jewellery of many multicoloured balls and baubles goes back into sectioned boxes. Slowly she is denuded, apart from the strings of lights twined around her slightly wilted frame. These are wound meticulously around their original cardboard holders. They must live to light another Christmas.

Finally the tree stands free of ornamentation. Somewhat less green than when she first arrived, the days of confinement have taken their toll. At the slightest touch she sheds a green shower of pine needles all around her. How to get her out of here without showering the whole house in a green carpet? The solution to this problem is a three-in-one job. The large pruner comes into play, and the tree is taken apart limb by limb. The limbs are pruned of their lesser limbs and cut into short sticks for the fire, while the little pine-needle ones are stacked into a bag and carried out to act as garden mulch in remote corners where they can compost in peace. The main trunk, still bearing the butt end of the branches, is set aside in a corner of the yard to join several companions from earlier Christmases to become a climber for roses or sweet pea in the summer. They are the ideal support for climbers as the stubs of the departed branches provide stepping stones for the greenery intent on making it to the top – a bit like the rock ledges that aid mountaineers to reach the summit. The entire tree is recycled to sustain the earth from whence it came, and the holly soon follows suit.

Gradually, the walls shed their ornamentation, which disappears into various boxes and returns to the press. The last man standing is the flamboyant Santa on top of the kitchen press, and when I reach up to tip him forward, he falls willingly down into my open arms. He bulges out of his box and has to be forced in. Could it be that from his high perch he has savoured the Christmas fare?

The last item to be packed away is the main crib. Eventually its turn comes, and by then the house seems incredibly clean and bare. That night, for the first time since the seventh of December when it was first switched on, the corner across the road is without our village Christmas tree, and the trees down along the street no longer glow with lights. Christmas is truly over.

Christmas fills a gap in the cold belly of winter. It serves a great need, providing a warm glow in the midst of dark days that enables us to step across the bridge from December into January. These are the two most challenging months of the year, and we need Christmas because without it the long grey days might be unendurable. From a rational and scientific point of view, there is no logic to Christmas. The practical amongst us would have us believe that it is in the sphere of fantasy and make-believe, the stuff that fairy tales are made of.

Christmas is a time to take stock and have a look at our world into which a new life has come. Most of us smile with delight when we see a baby. It brings out the best in us. The news of the birth of a baby brings a spontaneous rush of joy and renewed energy to all. Sometimes even the most troubled situations are calmed by the coming of a new baby, kindling the thought that it might be the time to make this world a better place for the newcomer. A new year has come and with it a sense of new beginnings. And, outside on the window sills, the boxes of primulas are glowing amidst the sprouting spring bulbs.

A Touch of Spring
Spring came today
And walked with me
Up the hill,
Breathing softness in the air,
Opening gates within my head.
The birds felt his presence,

Home for Christmas

Pouring forth symphonies
Of unrestrained welcome.
It was mid-January
And he just came
To have a peep,
Trailing behind him
Along the valley
Wisps of purple veils.